NEW DIRECTIONS FOR HIGHER EDUCATION

Martin Kramer
EDITOR-IN-CHIEF

The Professional School Dean: Meeting the Leadership Challenges

Michael J. Austin
University of California

Frederick L. Ahearn
Catholic University of America

Richard A. English
Howard University

EDITORS

Number 98, Summer 1997

JOSSEY-BASS PUBLISHERS
San Francisco

378.111
A937p
1997
FDC

THE PROFESSIONAL SCHOOL DEAN: MEETING THE
LEADERSHIP CHALLENGES
Michael J. Austin, Frederick L. Ahearn, Richard A. English (eds.)
New Directions for Higher Education, no. 98
Volume XXV, Number 2
Martin Kramer, Editor-in-Chief

ISSN 0271-0560   ISBN 0-7879-9849-4

NEW DIRECTIONS FOR HIGHER EDUCATION is part of The Jossey-Bass
Higher and Adult Education Series and is published quarterly by Jossey-
Bass Inc., Publishers, 350 Sansome Street, San Francisco, California
94104-1342. Periodicals postage paid at San Francisco, California, and at
additional mailing offices. POSTMASTER: Send address changes to New
Directions for Higher Education, Jossey-Bass Inc., Publishers, 350 Sansome Street, San Francisco, California 94104-1342.

SUBSCRIPTIONS cost $54.00 for individuals and $90.00 for institutions,
agencies, and libraries.

EDITORIAL CORRESPONDENCE should be sent to the Editor-in-Chief, Martin
Kramer, 2807 Shasta Road, Berkeley, California 94708-2011.

Cover photograph and random dot by Richard Blair/Color & Light © 1990.

Manufactured in the United States of America on Lyons Falls
Turin Book. This paper is acid-free and 100 percent totally
chlorine-free.

CONTENTS

Editors' Notes

The challenges facing university administrators have grown significantly with ever-increasing resource constraints. Although university and college presidents, provosts, and vice presidents for development carry the major responsibilities for educating the public and prospective donors about these constraints, the day-to-day management of the academic programs in higher education institutions is in the hands of deans. These academic leaders are the new senior managers in higher education. They are charged with assisting the faculty in maintaining high standards of teaching, scholarship, and community service while at the same time working with an array of stakeholders who include students, alumni, professional associations, accreditation bodies, deans in related schools, donors, and provosts.

The challenges facing professional school deans are the focus of this volume of New Directions for Higher Education, *The Professional School Dean: Meeting the Leadership Challenges.* The volume explores the wide range of leadership responsibilities faced by a professional school dean. Many of the case examples are drawn from the field of social work, but the contributors to this volume from the fields of engineering, law, nursing, and divinity found many parallels to their own experiences as dean of a professional school.

The contributions to this volume also reflect the significant shift over the past several decades in the role of the dean. Prior to the rapid expansion of higher education following World War II, the role of dean was patterned after the European tradition of elevating the most senior member of the faculty (often in Europe the only one holding the title of professor) to the position of dean for a term of office that might last decades. The dean was viewed as a leader among equals, based on seniority, maturity, and scholarly reputation. These expectations for the role of the dean changed dramatically as the size of universities grew rapidly and the complexity of the societal demands on institutions of higher education increased. The dean who served for twenty years became a rarity. The dean's role, especially in professional schools, began to change from the senior scholar in a school to a senior manager in the university. The chapters in this volume reflect some of the new demands on deans to engage in fundraising, serve as team leaders to facilitate faculty decision making, oversee expanding administrative support staff and facilities, initiate and maintain dialogue with the professional practice community, and continually search for new ways to respond as institutional leaders to the changing learning needs of students.

Definitions of a Dean

Morris (1981, p. 10) has observed that "Administrators are 51 percent born and 49 percent made. . . . deanly leadership, therefore, presents a special psychological burden. Although football teams recognize their need for a quarterback, academic faculties perpetuate the fantasy that they succeed more or less on their own. A dean must be able to live gracefully with that untruth." Because faculties actually believe that they do not need leadership, few faculty members begin their academic careers intending to become a dean. Moving from the ranks of the faculty to the university administration is generally considered an act of lunacy. Who would want to be a dean anyway? they ask. Thus, the acceptance of a deanship is often by chance and is occasioned usually by a colossal lack of knowledge of what the job entails.

What a dean actually does and the job requirements themselves may be mysterious to faculties, but administrators, who rely on the dean to carry out the mission, objectives, and policies of the university, are clear about it. In a classical sense, the dean is the ultimate middle manager—sandwiched between faculty and administration, answerable to the latter and always trying to please the former. The administration speaks—usually through the academic vice president or provost—in the form of specific expectations or marching orders: increase enrollment, strengthen the research and scholarly capacity of faculty, account for the school's budget, maintain the quality of the school's programs. The administration's expectations differ somewhat from the faculty's preoccupation with curricula, teaching, and research.

Faculties want a leader who gets resources for the school that lighten their workload—few or smaller classes, more time for research, and, of course, higher salaries. Faculties believe that the dean's principal duty is to serve their needs. Their perception of what a dean does often varies from that of the university administration's.

Other constituencies (students, alumni and alumnae, community agencies, and professional groups) have their own notions of what a dean is and does. The different definitions lead to obvious stresses and frequently to conflict. In addition, deans have a range of perceptions about what they do, which certainly influence the priorities they place on their activities and on the nature of their relationships.

Being dean of a professional school involves duties and activities that are more comprehensive than the chair of an arts and science department but less so than the duties of a provost or academic vice president. The activities include fundraising, student affairs, curriculum management, faculty personnel management, alumni and alumnae relations, supervision of administrative staff, media relations, facilities operation, contract negotiations, and grants management, to name a few.

The Art and Science of Deaning

Few deans have been trained in the "science" of higher education administration. Deans are, in most cases, individuals who have expertise in the discipline or profession of a department or school. Universities seldom look for managers or administrators who have been trained in the science of management or administration, except for specialized senior management positions such as finance, human resources, and development. The bias in selecting deans and provosts is definitely for an individual whose record of accomplishment in a discipline or profession includes teaching and research. Few professional managers become deans or provosts.

The dean also brings knowledge, skill, and experience, all of which have an impact on the organization's environment and culture. Some deans are asked to continue the status quo, but most are hired to bring about change through their vision of a new direction for the school. This vision must be compatible with the tradition and culture of the school even as it reflects new goals and objectives that could require new behaviors and interactions. As a dean enters a position of leadership (Austin, 1989), he or she is expected to inspire, motivate, and make decisions.

Although deans must acquire knowledge and skills in planning, budgeting, and evaluating programs, most of what deans do involves interaction with others. The dean's primary role is to nurture relationships that involve others in making decisions, determining goals and objectives, and designing and implementing policies and programs. As a supervisor, coach, mentor, and model for faculty and students, the dean seeks to inspire and motivate. A dean leads by encouraging the involvement of others. Faculty will take ownership when they have defined, planned, and developed a curriculum, policy, or program. The dean is also the arbitrator, mediator, advocate, and negotiator with the university administration. A dean must be attuned to interacting with faculty, students, administrators, alumni, and community constituencies.

Accepting a Deanship

At some point, an individual makes the decision to apply for a deanship. Some apply; others first get nominated then acquiesce to allowing their name to go forward in the search process. Either way, the hiring process soon leads to a list of finalists, interviews, and finally acceptance or rejection of an offer. Why would anyone go through this process? Why would anyone accept a deanship?

In each of the case studies that follow, the dean explored, directly and indirectly, the prospect of serving in academic administration for various professional and personal reasons. A career in academic administration is a challenge, either as an opportunity for career advancement or as a way to promote change. In the first instance, a deanship may be a goal of a senior faculty member who has experience as a program chair or coordinator, or perhaps as an assistant or associate dean. The deanship, then, is often the culmination of an academic career path. For a few others, the deanship may be a stop on the way to the post of academic vice president or the college presidency.

The opportunity for career advancement can be a major motivator because the job includes a higher salary and greater prestige than a faculty position. Deans, who usually have twelve-month contracts, are paid 10 to 50 percent more than senior faculty with nine-month contracts. Deans are among the highest-paid professionals in social work. The position can carry with it perks and benefits not available to faculty: reserved parking, larger offices, a personal travel budget, housing allowance in larger cities, and free entry into university events.

For others the deanship is an opportunity to promote change. The deans in this volume make clear that change is a high priority and is often related to research and scholarship, social justice, and educational innovation. Deans can achieve a change agenda with a vision that takes the school into new areas or necessitates changing the way things are done. An important strategy to achieve the changes discussed in these cases involves the hiring, firing, promoting, and tenuring of faculty. Personnel decisions can profoundly affect an academic unit. It can be argued that curriculum and research directions are determined by faculty personnel committees (for example, who gets hired directly affects what gets taught).

Stresses of Deaning

At the start of a deanship, there is usually a honeymoon period, during which all goes well. This is the time to introduce and carry out the change strategy, because invariably the new dean will face great pressures. The dean in one of the case studies arrived on campus and within six months was faced with the reaccreditation of the program. Although this provided an excellent opportunity to reassess program goals and objectives, it forced the new dean into a very time-consuming and labor-intensive activity at the expense of other significant administrative demands. Promoting faculty participation in the self-study process and working effectively with the site team that is evaluating the program requires considerable leadership from a dean.

Many new deans are unfamiliar with budget development and negotiations, and this can be a source of stress. Private universities may be chronically short of resources, and state universities have sustained massive cuts. As corporations and governments downsize, the university is the only major societal institution that has not been radically transformed. However, the pressures to reassess university structures and budgets are growing and will inevitably result in larger classes, more teaching hours, fewer grants for research, and less money for conference travel.

The dean feels the middle management budget squeeze between the university administration seeking cuts and the faculty seeking smaller classes, more support staff, more student financial aid, and more support for research and conference travel. When financial resources become scarce, the faculty frequently holds the dean responsible.

To the stress of budget reductions is added the pressure to raise funds to supplement student scholarships and support faculty activities and, in general, to advance the goals of the school. In private universities, particularly, there is an expectation that the school enroll enough students to cover all costs. The credo in many private universities of "every tub on its own bottom" requires each academic unit to fully support all of its activities. Public universities usually do not have these same fiscal pressures, but their enrollments may be capped until outside support for student aid and endowments is secured.

Most deans help to raise money for their schools. It is not unusual for a dean to be involved in writing grant proposals for a new building, establishing a scholarship fund for needy students, creating endowed chairs for distinguished faculty, funding school-community partnerships, or simply buying computers, carpeting, and furniture for the school's new building. Need always exceeds resources, and deans feel the tension of unmet demands.

Beyond the fiscal tensions of managing an educational and research program, the hiring and promotion decisions that prove, over time, to be wrong are the most painful to deans. When a new faculty member fails to develop and meet the requirements for promotion and tenure, it is difficult for the dean to deal with both the disappointed applicant for promotion and the rest of the faculty. Even more difficult are tenure and promotion decisions that are regretted later. In these cases, the dean and the institution must live with the decision that over a 30-year career could become a significant financial investment for the university.

Joys of Deaning

Great satisfaction can come from the accomplishments of a deanship. At a recent national conference of social work deans, a woman who had been a dean for 30 years said she was "very happy," citing the accomplishments of her faculty, the reputation of the school, and the respect from the university and the community. Another dean at that meeting said that being dean was "the best job" he ever had. Job satisfaction comes from being able to move a school into new areas, recruit better students and faculty, and increase the school's national and international reputation based on faculty research and other contributions to the profession. The status of the dean is enhanced by the contribution of everyone in the school's community.

The authors were also aware from the beginning of their administrative tenure that they would not be deans forever, so the question of "executive exit" was always present (Austin and Gilmore, 1992). It is not always clear when a dean should step down, retire, or move on. Each author struggled with the length of his term of office in a different way, and two had decided to step down or move on before this publication went to press. As is well known, deans who overstay their time in office can experience significant threats to their reputations. Planning the exit can be as important as the decision to accept a deanship.

Finally, in this volume are a number of suggestions for performing the duties and activities of a dean. They include such advice as always expect the unexpected, be an active listener, postpone important decisions to the next day, at times be vague with a "no comment," don't confuse the role of representing the university with personal entitlements, embrace fundraising as an essential part of the job, think big when it comes to setting a vision for the future, and replace antagonistic relationships with solid, working interactions. It is difficult for deans to do their jobs unless they first establish good relationships with the audiences to be served. It is important to know when the job is done and it is time to do something else, knowing that there will be recognition for one's achievements.

This volume seeks to provide "live reports from the front lines" of academic administration. It reflects three individuals' decisions to accept a deanship, and it documents their tasks, duties, and activities as it shares their stresses, pressures, accomplishments, and joys. The goal is to provide a set of perspectives on guiding organizational change while managing the role of dean.

The Chapters That Follow

The first chapter, by Fred Ahearn, paints a composite picture of a day in the life of a dean. The activities might actually be spread over a typical work week, but the intensity of moving from one activity to another throughout a given day is not unusual. It can appear exhausting and exhilarating, and frequently it is both. The goal of this chapter is to orient the reader to the array of issues confronting a dean as well as the many areas of responsibility that require both expertise and good judgment.

Chapter Two, by Richard English, is devoted to reflecting on the cross-cultural demands and expectations placed on a dean. Practitioners in professions such as engineering, nursing, and social work have developed their own ideas about what should be addressed in the curricula of a professional school and thereby reflect the culture of contemporary practice. On the other hand, the faculty in a professional school operates within the culture of academe and relates primarily to the expectations for quality teaching, scholarship, and community service. Communicating between these two cultures is one of the challenges faced by a professional school dean.

The third chapter, by the three editors of this volume, includes three case studies of very different schools of social work as illustrations of the different ways professional school deans seek to guide organizational change and transformation. In each case, there are vivid examples of the opportunities and threats to the organization, which can emerge from inside and outside the school. Building a shared vision and finding numerous opportunities to communicate it can be two of the major challenges facing a dean. Being open and optimistic in times of severe problems can tax the best of deans.

In Chapter Four, Mike Austin focuses on the immense need for peer support. Although it is not difficult to understand how lonely it can be at the top, it is not easy to find constructive and empowering ways to deal with the isolation. The ongoing self-assessment process is greatly enhanced if it is done with others who understand the role of the dean and are able to be supportive. Considerable attention is given in this chapter to the evolution of a dean's support group over a seven-year period.

The final chapters are devoted to the reactions and comments of several colleagues who either have served as a dean or are currently in that role. The goal of these chapters is to tap the perspectives of others whose deanship was influenced by different organizational, geographic, political, economic, or cultural factors. They provide an opportunity to validate common experiences as well as to identify significant differences that might affect a dean's performance.

Chapter Five, by Rino Patti, addresses the importance of knowledge development as part of the culture of a professional school. This is a critical issue given the pressure on professional school faculty to educate skilled practitioners for the field while at the same time responding to the norms of academe related to scholarly productivity. In Chapter Six, Stuart Kirk helps all current and future deans recognize that their leadership impact may be either overly inflated or unknown when viewed through the eyes of faculty. Chapter Seven, by Paula Allen-Meares, highlights the challenges facing deans in large public universities with special attention to career development and the unique experiences of women.

In Chapter Eight, Tom Ehrlich focuses on some of the issues buried in the relationship between the dean and provost based on his experiences in both roles, as well as his perspective as a former university president. Chapter Nine, by Claire Fagin, addresses the importance of the dean's role in the community as an advocate for her professional school along with the joys of the deanship role. In Chapter Ten, Clarence Newsome confronts the question of what a dean actually does as a leader day in and day out. And in the concluding Chapter Eleven, John McCoy identifies the leadership demands on a dean who advocates for change based on the changing needs of his profession and the society at large.

This volume is first and foremost a labor of love written by academic administrators who thrived on the challenges and lived to tell about them. Busy administrators rarely have the time or inclination to reflect on their experiences in writing, so it is our hope that our experiences and the reflections of others will be helpful to those who aspire to the challenging leadership role of the professional school dean.

Michael J. Austin
Frederick L. Ahearn
Richard A. English
Editors

References

Austin, M. J. "Executive Entry: Multiple Perspectives on the Process of Muddling Through." *Administration in Social Work*, 1989, *13* (4), 55–71.

Austin, M. J., and Gilmore, T. "Executive Exit: Multiple Perspectives on Managing the Leadership Transition." *Administration in Social Work*, 1992, *17* (1), 47–60.

Morris, V. C. *Deaning: Middle Management in Academe.* Urbana, Ill.: University of Illinois, 1981.

MICHAEL J. AUSTIN is professor in the School of Social Welfare at the University of California, Berkeley and dean emeritus of the School of Social Work at the University of Pennsylvania.

FREDERICK L. AHEARN is professor and dean emeritus at the National School of Social Services, Catholic University of America, Washington, D.C.

RICHARD A. ENGLISH is dean of the School of Social Work at Howard University, Washington, D.C.

Some call deaning a rat race; others refer to it as all in a day's work.

A Day in the Life of a Dean

Frederick L. Ahearn

Driving to work today is not typical. The soft breeze carries the aroma of spring's first flowers, now in full bloom. Winter's dreariness is finally over. It is amazing how wonderful one feels on a day like this. A radio commentator's familiar voice is in the background: "Morning Edition" has become my daily driving companion as well as my prime source of news. I begin to think of my schedule today at the university, especially how I will deal with the academic vice president during our midmorning appointment. More about that later.

As I enter the campus, I am struck by its beauty, its greenery, the tulips, and the old, stately buildings. Few students are around, and I remember how I, too, used to prefer to study late at night and not start my day early in the morning. Soon the campus will be bustling as students hurry from class to class. This is also the time new students and their parents visit the campus to make their final decision on which college to attend in the fall. I am sure that they are just as impressed as I am with the beauty of this morning and our campus.

So another day begins, and my agenda, as usual, is full. Sometimes I wonder if my life has become one long meeting. Fitting things into my schedule is becoming a juggling act—so much to do in so little time. In the pages that follow, I will paint a verbal portrait of a typical day in my life as dean of the graduate school of social work at a private, medium-sized urban university.

8:00 A.M.: Mail, Letters, Reports, and Time to Think

When I arrive at my office, I tackle my mail, already sorted by my director of administration. Today I encounter fourteen letters from individuals and organizations, a normal amount of mail. After a cup of coffee, I dig into the stack.

NEW DIRECTIONS FOR HIGHER EDUCATION, no. 98, Summer 1997 © Jossey-Bass Publishers

First I open a notice of a meeting on professional licensing to be held next month; next is a call for papers to be presented at next year's meeting of the National Conference on Aging; then a request by a doctoral student in Colorado to survey master's programs about the effect of their curricula on disabled persons. I send the meeting announcement to the clinical faculty with a short memorandum; on the call for papers I write "post"; the survey request I refer to the associate dean, who also directs the master's program. I quickly dispense with the other announcements and requests, referring them to the proper persons, posting them, or tossing them in the trash.

I am pleasantly surprised to open a card from a 1936 alumna of the program who had enclosed a $2,000 check for our department's seventy-fifth anniversary celebration. I draft a warm response, thanking her for her generosity and inviting her to attend the anniversary dinner to be held in the fall. And, because I have been working with the development office to plan a fundraising campaign during our seventy-fifth year, I send over the name and address of this alumna, who might consider another gift next year.

The next letter is not so pleasant. An angry student complains that she is not able to register for an elective course that her faculty adviser has recommended she take: "With the high tuition that students must pay today, the school should have extra sections of the important courses that students need for their professional training." In reply, I indicate that the school cannot add another section because of recent budget cuts, that registration for all courses is on a first-come, first-served basis, and that the elective in question is offered each summer and fall. I suggest that she consult with her faculty adviser to review other elective options at the school or at other schools in the university.

Also in the mail today is a request for proposal from the U.S. Department of Education for the Patricia Roberts Harris Fellowship Program. Each of the past five years we have received Harris grants to recruit minority students for careers that lead to public service and leadership. As a private university, our tuition is very high, and the Harris fellowships allow us to recruit individuals who otherwise could not afford to attend our school. Because this opportunity to add to our program's diversity is a real plus for us, I jot a note asking one of our faculty members to revise our proposal and increase our request by six more full scholarships before the due date of May 15.

The next item in front of me is a request to pay the annual dues for our school's membership in the American Public Welfare Association, which provides leadership on issues of income maintenance and security. The association's program and legislative information are considered useful by our social policy professors. I know that resources like this must now be considered a luxury. In this time of fiscal austerity, I must make some difficult choices, and discontinuing our membership in this important organization is one of the sacrifices I have to make. The request ends up in the wastebasket.

Just then, Maria comes into my office to clean the bathroom and empty the trash. A refugee from Nicaragua, she and her husband came here six years ago to avoid the civil war in their country and to look for a better way of life for themselves and their children. Each morning she knocks at my office door as she enters, asking "Como estás, Señor?" It has become a ritual to stop for a few minutes to hear the latest from Maria about her work or her family. On this day, she tells me she cannot get time off from work to keep her appointment with her doctor, and she asks if I would call to cancel the appointment, as the doctor's receptionist does not understand Spanish. Our brief morning meetings have helped me to keep up on my Spanish fluency, and I agree to make the call.

Once Maria leaves, I finish the mail and take a few minutes to scan the *Chronicle of Higher Education*. This is a luxury for me, though I enjoy reading about the current issues in higher education, learning what foundations are funding, and checking to see which positions in my field are being advertised. But I can only scan the headlines before I check my calendar for the day and make notes for each of my scheduled meetings.

9:00 A.M.: Dean's Secretary and the Director of Administration

As Mary, my secretary, and Joyce, the director of administration, arrive at work, we meet for a few minutes to review what we accomplished yesterday and what we have before us today. Mary says she has finished typing up the notes from the last meeting of the Committee on Appointments and Promotion and the report is ready for my signature before she sends it to the academic senate for action. I give her the mail that I have just reviewed, and we discuss some other assignments and my calendar for the day. I ask her to be alert for a call I am expecting from the dean of the University of Pennsylvania, about a paper we are writing, and tell her to interrupt me if necessary when the call comes.

Joyce briefs me on the plans for registration for both the summer session and the fall term. She has already spoken with the program chairs about the number of sections in certain courses and put in a request with the university for extra classrooms. We have just converted to telephone registration, and procedures have been worked out for students to see their advisers for course planning and for obtaining their personal identification number, which is required to access the new registration procedure from the university's computer. I remind her to get the names of all the adjunct faculty who teach in the summer session and to prepare their contracts for my signature.

Mary and Joyce will check with me throughout the day to update me on specific items and to ask for my advice on pending matters. This is almost always done ad hoc between appointments. My next appointment is with the academic vice president in his office.

9:10 A.M.: Academic Vice President

I approach this appointment with dread. The academic vice president (AVP) and I do not get along well. Dr. Peter Smith has never been a dean, and I feel strongly that he cannot effectively represent the needs of the deans to the administration. His top-down model of management often fails to include the perspective and participation of the schools. That style is difficult for me to work with, and even after four years of working with him, I find the atmosphere during our meetings tense.

As usual, our meeting starts out with very little personal talk, and I find myself adopting a formal manner: "Peter, I sent you a tentative agenda by fax yesterday. I need your advice and your decision concerning next year's budget, the school's plans for its seventy-fifth anniversary, and the sharing of indirect costs from funded grants. Also, I'd like to bring you up to date on our current enrollment picture for next year."

Most of our discussion revolves around financial problems. First, I bring up the notice I received that the school's budget would be cut 1 percent next year, the second consecutive year of requested budget decreases. The AVP reminds me that some other schools are suffering worse cuts. He adds, "Our cuts are nothing like those that public universities have had to face." It is apparent to me that the door is closed on this topic, so I conclude by telling him I am considering deleting a secretarial position to meet the budget-cut request. I add that I have consulted my school management team and we will make the final decision within a few days.

Moving to another fiscal matter, I ask Peter for his decision on my request for a special budget supplement of $9,650 to support the activities of the school's seventy-fifth anniversary celebration. The AVP's response is brief: "I don't have the money in my budget. Can you take it from yours?" There is no flexibility in the school's budget, I quickly retort. He closes the topic tersely: "I'm sorry; there's no money."

Our next exchange concerns yet another financial matter. Over the years, it has been customary for promoted faculty to get a 10 percent raise, with the funds coming from the AVP's office. I ask for the approximately $3,600 additional for the member of my faculty who has just been promoted to associate professor. He says he cannot cover the expenditure this year and that I should meet this obligation from my budget. When I object, he orders me to pay for the raise from other areas of the school's budget.

Our final fiscal item brings another disappointment. I ask for a small percentage of the indirect cost monies that are generated by the grants that the school brings into the university. It is common knowledge on campus that some units as well as several "superstar" faculty have negotiated with the university administration for the return of 10 percent of the indirect cost funds. Over the past year, I have made this request several times, but never received a response to my memoranda. The atmosphere is still tense from our previous budget discussion, and the AVP is curt: "The request is under review. Therefore, no decision will be made until the executive vice president has decided on the matter."

"Peter," I protest, "let me bring you up to date with our enrollment prospects for next year," and then I proceed to explain how that mitigates any request for funds. Applications exceed last year's by 26 percent and actual paid applications already exceed our enrollment targets for next year, I note, and I remind him that the school has substantially increased its contribution to the university during the past three years while enrollments at other units in the university have been dropping dramatically. In fact, I point out, the School of Social Welfare in the past two years has realized increases of 12 percent and 9 percent in student enrollments. Although I stress the school's contribution to the university, I make it clear that we cannot accept more students unless there is more money for adjunct faculty.

Finally, the AVP agrees that if we bring in an additional fifteen full-time students, he will provide an extra $21,000 for faculty. I know that such an increase in enrollment will bring in more than $200,000 to the university in additional tuition, and I feel—but do not express—resentment about the discrepancy. He probably resents my quid pro quo approach to the issue.

As I walk back to my office, I think about how much more difficult it is to be a dean when you have to cut a budget that is already inadequate, and when the AVP has little regard for the school. I have always tried to emphasize how the school contributes to the university and its mission, but I feel that the AVP does not understand the school or its mission. Perhaps some of his actions and perceptions were due to our poor relationship.

Walking back to my office, I don't even notice the tulips.

10:00 A.M.: Faculty Plans

As I enter my office, Mary tells me that Mike Barrett, an assistant professor, is waiting to see me. Mike has been at the school three years teaching in the master's program. Each faculty member at the beginning of the academic year sets goals in the areas of teaching, service, and scholarship. This meeting with Mike is an opportunity to assess how well he has accomplished his goals.

Mike and I socialize a bit, then discuss his achievements for the year. We review his course evaluations, noting the scores given by the students and their comments. Mike is a gifted teacher: he carefully prepares for his classes, makes time available to meet with students, and takes pride in his work. Students like and respect him. We discuss his interest in the doctoral program, and I suggest that he consider becoming a reader on a dissertation. I commend Mike for his excellent teaching and encourage him to read his course evaluations and set new teaching goals for the next semester.

Mike has demonstrated similar success in the second required area: service to the school, the university, and the larger community. We talk briefly about his activities on the Admissions Committee and the Minority Students Committee. He is committed to the recruitment of minorities to the school, and he helped design a recruitment plan for the Office of Admissions. He makes himself available to meet with minority students who apply for admission and generously gives time to the Minority Students Committee.

My only concern about Mike's performance is in the area of research. He works hard at his research, but has published only one refereed journal article.

With only three years to go before tenure review, he has to place greater emphasis on his scholarly work and writing because a faculty member is expected to produce a minimum of five publications before seeking promotion and tenure. I suggest he work with a senior faculty member, someone with a similar scholarly interest who has published widely. Mike likes this approach. We also talk about submitting a paper to a professional conference and about applying to the university for a small grant that would allow him to pursue a new research interest. Mike agrees to apply for the grant and to focus on research and writing for next year.

The aspect of my work that involves supporting the development of young faculty members is the most satisfying for me, and I conclude this meeting with a sense of accomplishment and joy in seeing Mike's progress and achievements, although I worry about his limited progress in publishing.

10:30 A.M.: Student Association

As Mike leaves my office, Mary informs me that the Student Association leaders will be about five minutes late for our regular weekly meeting. This gives me a chance to sign a few letters that Mary has prepared and to return several phone calls.

Four students join me in my office and begin by telling me that they wish to discuss elective courses, selection of practica, scheduling of courses, and graduation.

"Dean, we pay very high tuition here and think we should be able to have the courses we need to be successful in our field," they say. Students today compare themselves to customers and believe that the quality of the product (courses) should be commensurate with the price (tuition). In this instance, they want me to add several sections of the most popular elective courses. Just as I have done earlier in the morning when answering a student's letter, I explain the school's limitation in adding course sections: money. I agree to ask the associate dean and chair of the master's program if a neighboring school has the courses and space available (all the universities in the area have an arrangement that permits students from one university to take courses at another without additional cost).

The student leaders move on to the subject of student selection of the required field practicum. Their concerns are serious. They criticize the paucity of placements, the way a certain faculty member treats students, and the lack of information about the options. In response, I promise to investigate the matter with the associate dean and the director of field and report back to them next week.

The Student Association leaders remind me that half of the students in the master's program attend school part-time. For these students, taking classes during the day is often difficult because of work schedules, day care arrangements, or other family responsibilities. They want the school to consider offering some required courses in the evening. This seems reasonable, and I promise to check on the feasibility of revising some course time schedules. I agree to review the matter with the associate dean and have a response by our next weekly meeting.

With respect to graduation, the student leaders have polled the graduating class and are recommending that the director of the local AIDS support service be the graduation speaker. Knowing this person's work and excellent reputation, I readily agree to ask him.

Our meeting ends cordially, and we tentatively agree to meet the next week at the same time. I reflect briefly on the satisfaction I get from interacting with students—a favorite part of my responsibilities.

11:00 A.M.: Associate Dean

My regular meeting with the associate dean is next, so the students' issues can get immediate attention. We try to meet at this time every week, though other pressures sometimes interfere. We check in with each other for a few minutes almost every day, but those on-the-run conversations are usually brief. This is Dr. Beverly Hutchins' first year as associate dean, and I am finding her to be an invaluable help to me. She was promoted to associate professor with tenure last year and, though eligible for a sabbatical, has agreed to accept the associate deanship for a two-year period. In this position, she is chair of the master's degree program, the school's largest component, and her responsibilities also include coordinating the activities of the baccalaureate, master's, and doctoral programs. She runs the management team meetings, prepares a draft of the faculty workload assignments, coordinates the work of the administrative assistants, and supervises the director of the Office of Field. Of course, in addition, Dr. Hutchins serves as dean in my absence.

Beverly is a hard worker and a good administrator. She is deeply loyal, expresses her views very frankly, and possesses a great sense of humor. Her colleagues respect her and find it easy to approach her about their concerns. She struggles to be available to each of us, but like many faculty today, feels torn between her administrative duties and the need to attend to her scholarship and her family.

Our discussion focuses on routine topics such as the plans for the upcoming preregistration. She has worked with Joyce to revise some of the procedures, and everything seemed to be in place. We also talk about the final review of students who plan to graduate in May. Several have been in academic difficulty, and they will be assessed by the Master's Review Committee. The students have consulted her about the graduation speaker, and she also approves of the choice.

I summarize my meeting with the Student Association leaders and ask Dr. Hutchins to follow up on the matters of evening courses and the problems associated with the selection of the field practicum. We also discuss whether she can sit in on my next meeting with the student leaders.

11:30 A.M.: Meeting with a Major Donor

As I open my office door, I am greeted by Dr. Stephen Nash, vice president for development. With him is Everrett Hightower, a trustee of the university and a successful Pennsylvania businessman. Hightower is very interested in the plight of the homeless and wants to know what the school is doing on this front. Dr. Nash has told him a little of our involvement with homeless concerns and also about our seventy-fifth anniversary celebration. Dr. Nash has told me earlier that Hightower is considering giving $1 million to the university and that there is a good chance he may donate the same amount to the school. Dr. Nash opens the meeting with a brief explanation of why we have gotten together.

Hightower is friendly and outgoing, and he seems genuinely interested in the school's activities. I describe our Project Connect, through which students perform their field internship at a local woman's shelter. The project connects women to the resources they need to become independent. Six graduate students contribute twenty hours a week for two semesters, a substantial form of assistance to a local agency that lacks services to assist homeless women.

Hightower expresses interest in the annual conference that we cosponsor on topics that concern the homeless. I tell him about one conference, a gathering of bankers, developers, social workers, city officials and workers, and religious leaders to consider ways to build single-room housing for the homeless. Another conference focused on how to build into existing programs "a service-enriched approach" to help the homeless achieve independence. Hightower shows great interest and asks to be invited to the next one.

In closing, Hightower asks what we need most—what we would get if we had extra money. I expected this question and quickly tell him of three ideas. First, triple the size of Project Connect as a way to reach hundreds of homeless in the city. Second, develop a research fund so faculty could study the many questions and solutions to the problem. Third, establish an endowed chair on homelessness and issues of social justice. He nods in agreement; he is fascinated.

They leave, and I am left with the feeling that we have a good chance to receive a large gift.

12:15 P.M.: Lunch at the City Department of Social Services

I rush out of the office to attend a luncheon at our local Department of Social Services, which is very close to the university. The purpose of the luncheon is to meet with the commissioner and her management team to discuss a federal entitlement program, Title IV-E, in hopes of bringing millions of dollars to the city to train child welfare workers. I arrive, and I am led into a small conference room. After helping myself to my usual salad, the meeting begins.

Commissioner Jane Laddin is new to the area, and this is the second time we have met. At the first meeting, she asked if I would return to speak to her leadership staff about the ins and outs of the Title IV-E legislation. I proceed to give a fifteen-minute talk about the history of this legislation, citing the benefits of the program. I explain that a university, in collaboration with a local Department of Social Services, can apply for an entitlement from the U.S. Department of Health and Human Services. The entitlement, which could add up to thousands of dollars, would pay for the orientation, training, and advancement of workers who deliver social services to children and their families, especially in the city's child welfare system. The university puts up 25 percent of the funds, almost always through in-kind contributions, which then are matched by a 75 percent contribution from the federal government. The city would be the beneficiary of a training program delivered by the local university and completely funded with outside money.

After a lively discussion and a number of questions, it is decided that a planning committee of representatives from the local universities and the Department of Social Services be set up to prepare a plan of action and a proposal. I support the decision, say goodbye, and then race back to the office.

1:30 P.M.: Conference Call

Mary knocks at my door to announce that the scheduled 1:30 conference call is on time. As a member of the Executive Committee of the National Conference on Aging, I am frequently involved in discussions about the organization's finances, goals, and personnel. This call is to discuss the feasibility of setting up an endowment fund to support gerontological research. The NCOA president may be able to obtain a large gift for this purpose, and he wants to consult with the eight-member Executive Committee. After much comment complicated by having eight individuals all trying to participate in one telephone conversation, we vote to approve the plan and proceed with setting up the endowment.

2:00 P.M.: Committee on Appointments and Promotion

I have just enough time before my next meeting to call back the development director to answer a question about the campaign we are planning for the school's seventy-fifth anniversary. He wants the names of alumni who could serve as a fundraising committee, and he makes it clear that he hopes to connect this activity to his university fundraising effort.

The five members of the school's Committee on Appointment and Promotion (CAP), all senior faculty, enter as I finish my phone call. As dean, I am an ex officio member of this committee, and I chair the meetings. However, I do not vote with the CAP; I express my vote separately on each matter that comes before the committee. Our task today is to review the materials of an assistant professor who has applied for promotion and tenure.

The CAP members all agree that this candidate is an excellent teacher. His student evaluations contain such phrases as "knows his subject," "master communicator," and "always there for the students." He has developed several new courses and written a section of the accreditation self-study pertaining to his area of expertise. There is disagreement, however, about this professor's scholarship.

"Thirty-seven pages of published materials is hardly enough to qualify," one CAP member comments. Another observes that the applicant has published in the best journals in the field. The dispute continues as another member describes the input from six reviewers outside the school who have questioned the quality of the articles. "Look," says still another CAP member, "the candidate is a great teacher and has a record of service to the school. There's enough in the way of research to gain our approval." The disagreement continues for over an hour as the five faculty members fight over the credentials of the candidate. Conflicts lead to loss of temper, which results in personal insults. Finally, a vote is taken: three to two in favor of promotion and tenure. More seriously, however, is the anger, distrust, and hostility the meeting has engendered. This is the first time that some latent negative feelings among the members have become overt, and there is nothing that I could have done to mediate successfully between the warring parties.

I finally end the meeting knowing that this split will continue to interfere with other business in the school. How will I be able to manage these differences? How can I breach the differences and negotiate a compromise? I will have to end up siding with one group over the other. I am disgusted!

3:30 P.M.: Children's Hospital Director of Social Services

Larry Madden, director of social services at our local hospital center, is waiting for me as I arrive ten minutes late for our meeting. We begin to discuss what I call "a university-community partnership." For some time, I have been working on the details of a collaboration between a community-based agency and our faculty and students to develop innovative approaches to practice, research, and training.

Such a partnership could serve many purposes: faculty are always interested in opportunities that could lead to research and publication possibilities; practitioners are concerned about solving the tough practice issues that they face day in and day out; and students want a field practicum that exposes them to the latest knowledge and skills in their field.

Larry and I have already taken some concrete steps toward the partnership. We have each named a lead person to explore the details of the collaboration, and twelve of his staff have joined in meetings with eight of my faculty. They have formed nine teams around specific practice issues and planned to apply for demonstration funds to try new approaches and to evaluate the results. Several of the students placed with the agency have also participated in the planning and become part of the demonstration and research groupings.

As our meeting ends, I tell Larry—citing the school's work with his agency as a model—that the faculty have recommended that the school pursue partnerships with community agencies. Faculty are enthusiastic at the prospect of joint research projects, especially if the projects are funded. I know, of course, that there will come a time when faculty will want workload credit for this work even though they have a "research day" in their weekly schedule to pursue scholarly work.

4:00 P.M.: Alumni Planning Committee for the School's Seventy-Fifth Anniversary

I hurry to the faculty conference room to participate with the alumni in planning the school's seventy-fifth anniversary celebration. "Hello, Dean," comes from every direction. I greet individuals as I work my way around the room. About twenty-four alums are in attendance (very good, I think, for a third meeting), standing about the room chatting and drinking refreshments.

"Well, let's get started," I say.

At this meeting we are to hear from each of the subcommittees about an element of the plan for the celebration. Earlier, we have decided to have a year-long celebration with events that will bring graduates back to the school and also involve members of the professional community. People are in good spirits, obviously enthusiastic about what we are doing. The reports begin, with the subcommittee chair leading the discussion on each topic. The specific plans include

- Opening dinner and honors ceremony
- Development campaign to raise $750,000
- Monthly seminar series on professional topics, each followed by a reception
- Two major educational events for students
- Key alums or notables in the profession for honorary degrees or Presidential Medals

As the decisions are made on each of these items, I think that this is indeed an excellent meeting and that the seventy-fifth anniversary celebration will have many benefits for the school.

"Thanks to each of you. You have been a big help," I comment.

"Let us know if you plan another meeting," advises one alumna.

"The next step is to ask our public relations office to prepare a brochure for us containing a list of the events, dates, places, and so forth. We'll do a mailing on September first. Each subcommittee will be responsible for its event, and I will meet with that group a short time before. The committee on the fundraising will continue meeting as usual," I conclude.

Some hurry out the door, but many stay around and chat. They seem happy to be back at the school and to see old friends.

Driving home this night, I feel tired. I am not happy with my meetings with the academic vice president and the senior faculty on the Committee on Appointment and Promotion, but the enthusiasm, ideas, and decisions of the alums have made me feel that the seventy-fifth anniversary celebration will be a success. As I reminisce about the day's happenings, I become conscious of a news report about problems in the Middle East. It is "All Things Considered," and this is my usual way of unwinding before arriving home for dinner. After all, it is spring and the tulips and other flowers are in full bloom. I can smell the floral aroma as I leave the campus. This concludes another day in the life of a dean.

FREDERICK L. AHEARN is professor and dean emeritus at the National School of Social Services, Catholic University of America, Washington, D.C.

The ultimate town-gown distinction is reflected in the off-campus culture of practicing professionals and the on-campus culture of academics. The professional school dean must bridge the gap.

The Deanship as a Cross-Cultural Experience

Richard A. English

Professional school deans must be bicultural. They belong to the institutional culture of the university and to the culture of their profession in the larger society. Coping with these complementary and conflicting cultures requires an unusual balancing act for a deanship to succeed. Henry Rosovsky (1987), the former dean of the faculty of arts and sciences at Harvard University, points out that an arts and sciences dean must face responsibilities unrelated to any standard description of a profession or discipline. In contrast, deans of medicine, law, and social work continue to function as doctors, lawyers, and social workers. For Rosovsky, arts and sciences are not subjects and deaning is strictly administrative, with very little to do with one's own academic discipline. This is not the case for professional school deans.

This chapter focuses on a range of cross-cultural experiences related to building bridges between such differing cultures as the arts and sciences orientation of universities and the service orientation of professional schools, the academic orientation of professional schools and the pragmatic orientation of community agencies, basic science disciplines and applied science professions on campus, university promotion criteria, definitions of citizenship or community service, and one's own acculturation in academe and the profession. The chapter concludes with some lessons learned in managing cross-cultural expectations and communications.

To understand the cross-cultural dimensions of deaning requires a few working definitions. First, *culture* consists of the institutions, patterns of interaction, and mental attitudes that form the social life of a community. The *community*, in our analysis, consists of the academic community of a professional school, the broader university community, and the professional practitioner community. It represents a collection of shared interests, norms, and ways of interacting. In this context, culture is viewed as the glue that holds the community together and provides meaning, cohesion, and integration.

Second, because the dean deals with a number of communities, each with its own culture, the role calls for multicultural capacities to provide links between and within each culture. For example, helping a university provost who might have been educated as a research physicist to understand the role of a profession requires the same type of multicultural communication skills as helping the practice community understand the role of professional school faculty in a research university.

Third, deans play a role in influencing cultures by seeking to modify existing cultures and create new cultures. Developing a vision of the future for a school or setting goals and priorities are actions designed in one way or another to influence, change, or create cultures. In so doing, deans might introduce changes in patterns of daily interaction, restructure jobs that require changes in personal behavior, and develop new definitions of expected and acceptable behavior. To be an agent of cultural change, a new dean, especially one who is appointed from the outside, must understand the host culture as well as his or her own values, beliefs, and leadership style, because all play a role in the dean's strategies for cultural change.

When moving outside the school into the broader university and the practice community, the dean's cross-cultural communications skills are continually tested. To communicate effectively with the university's academic administrators as well as with those responsible for finance, buildings, public relations, student affairs, development, or alumni relations, the dean must understand multiple cultures, because miscommunication and conflict can erupt at a moment's notice. This cross-cultural intermediary role requires a working knowledge of fundamentally different individual and group values, expectations, and patterns of behavior, because the representatives of these different cultures—such as provosts, financial officers, and development officers—can support or create stress for a professional school.

The cross-cultural opportunities in the practice community and the community at large can also be multifaceted for a dean. Connecting with practitioners, governmental agencies, foundations, and advocacy groups of all kinds may involve the dean in serving as a volunteer, a university representative to contract negotiations, a defendant in legal action, or as the recipient of constructive criticism from the practice community. Whatever the role, communicating across different cultures requires multicultural knowledge and understanding. For example, members of the professional practice community need to understand that deans do not fire faculty members. A knowledge of the process of faculty recruitment, appointment, and tenure is a process that includes the dean, the faculty, the chief academic officer of the university, the president, and the board of trustees.

Continuous interaction or exchange between cultures can lead to acculturation. Evidence of this process can be seen in the change and in the adoption of different values, norms, expectations, and behaviors. The essential question for the dean to answer relates to whether the dean has acculturated to the school or whether the school and its stakeholders have adapted to the leadership and management style of the dean.

Professional school deans need to be skilled in administration and in their academic disciplines. They also must understand university policies and practices within the higher education culture. Exchanges between universities and external bodies such as state legislatures, regulatory agencies, accreditation bodies, federal agencies, and foundations are often complex, sometimes intrusive, processes critical to institutional viability.

Reading the literature on higher education differs from reviewing the research literature of one's own field. Understanding national higher education issues is essential to appreciate what might be going on on one's own campus. For example, the *Chronicle of Higher Education* newspaper can help a dean understand the viewpoints of the higher education community.

Culture of Tenure and Promotion

There was a time in many professions when practitioners were educated outside the university in independent schools or training centers. The promotion of professional education as a component of university life can be seen in the histories of most professions, such as hospital-based nursing education or agency-based social work education. Although the transition from community to campus created great tension between fledgling professions and the university, development of the profession, with respect to scientific inquiry and teaching, came to depend on its location in the academy rather than in the community. Universities require, to this day, that faculty who wish to remain in good standing engage in research and teaching, not in providing services in the community.

Among the critical areas of potential conflict between university administration and professional school administration, the most troublesome is probably the appointment, promotions, and tenure process. Tensions usually arise around the university's research and peer-reviewed publications criteria for promotion and tenure and the demands of managing a professional school.

Unlike faculty in other department disciplines, who can devote themselves primarily to teaching and research, professional school faculty are expected to teach, conduct research, advise students, maintain periodic contact between the practice community and their students, serve on school and university committees, and be active in both professional and community service. The demands and expectations placed on the professional school scholar, therefore, are many and varied, often in conflict with each other and frequently time-consuming. Some faculty sacrifice research, writing, and other scholarly tasks to the plethora of responsibilities related to keeping the professional school afloat.

The expectation is that faculty will perform well in all areas. In reality, this is not the case. Typically, faculty members who perform exceptionally well in knowledge development, research, and teaching are not heavily involved in the maintenance of the educational enterprise. Good teachers who spend an inordinate amount of time counseling students, serving on school committees, and carrying out other maintenance tasks, usually are not engaged in research. At the time of promotion and tenure, when a rigorous test for research and publication is applied, the dedicated faculty member who has not been involved in knowledge development is unable to meet the promotion and tenure requirements.

The dean is torn between the faculty members, who view the candidate for tenure as a valued colleague worthy of promotion and tenure, and his or her own evaluation, which may agree with the faculty's but places a higher value on the research and publication requirement. This situation generally is further complicated by the provost or chief academic officer, who views the granting of tenure as a major economic investment for the university.

Deans approach tenure and promotion differently from faculty and administrators. These differences largely reflect organizational policies and practices, circumstances in the university and school, and management styles of the deans. In some cases, deans differ with the faculty committee's recommendation and help convince the chief academic officer to deny tenure and promotion. In most cases, however, the deans become actively involved in nurturing the careers of new faculty members to ensure their success in teaching, research, and service. When a faculty member does not receive approval for tenure and promotion, it is usually an emotional and painful experience for all parties. In some cases, it is akin to a separation or death in a family. Bringing the faculty together after the termination of a faculty member is a major test of a dean's leadership skills.

It is important to note that tenure and promotion issues represent but a small component of a dean's efforts to foster faculty development in a highly individualistic culture. Performance is assessed primarily on an individual's creativity, energy, and productivity, but for most deans, guiding organizational change through the involvement and support of faculty begins with recruitment. As vacancies are announced and candidates are screened, deans work closely with their faculty personnel committees to clarify the expectations for a position, explore the fit between applicants' unique characteristics and the school's needs and expectations, and encourage careful scrutiny of applicants' references and on-campus visitations. When faculty complete their peer review assessment of applicants, with or without ranking the leading candidates, most deans view faculty recommendations as advisory in order to maintain management's prerogative in the hiring process. If the process has been thorough and the pool of finalists are highly competent, the dean's choices can be easy. If, on the other hand, the competence level is low but the faculty is clamoring to fill the position to lighten course loads and university administrators are worrying about the potential loss of the faculty line, the dean can experience intense resentment if he or she decides that none of the finalists are satisfactory and extends the search into the next academic year.

Enhancing the culture of faculty support for research can further challenge deans seeking to promote organizational change. Giving junior faculty released time to strengthen their scholarly record can unleash senior faculty resentment if their committee work increases as a result. Or it might stir personal memories of inadequate administrative support when they were up for tenure twenty or thirty years earlier. The senior faculty subculture represents yet another major challenge for deans. This challenge includes balancing teaching and administrative responsibilities for senior faculty who are no longer actively producing scholarship, engaging in highly sensitive and emotionally charged topics such as retirement planning, and finding ways to encourage and support senior faculty in their mentoring roles with junior, nontenured faculty.

One big challenge to deans seeking to create a better balance between the school's commitment to quality professional education and the faculty's investment in an active program of research is to find ways to help the faculty build ongoing programs of research. Deans are often confronted with the power of the professional education culture, which usually emphasizes teaching at the expense of creating a parallel culture of research and scholarship.

The process of rebalancing the emphasis between education and research can be a source of significant tension that affects the climate and culture of a school. The demands placed on junior faculty to engage in research can be easily aggravated by senior faculty who do not share the new values for balance. Although the dean's primary focus is on assisting junior faculty achieve success in research, teaching, and community service, it is also necessary to address the need for group support by creating a culture of research collaboration within the school and with joint appointments outside the school. For example, in one of the schools described in Chapter Three of this volume, the dean sought to alter the culture of the school by creating joint appointments for research with local community organizations. The faculty job announcement indicated that participating faculty members' teaching loads would be reduced by one-third to accommodate the community-based research program to be developed for the benefit of the faculty, the organization, and the school. Some of the junior faculty who assumed those new roles achieved success in conducting exploratory research as well as initiating funded research; others found the adaptation to two cultures (university and agency) too difficult to manage.

As professional school deans attempt to guide organizational change, sensitivity to the school's culture is essential. Helping a group to address changing organizational priorities challenges any administrator. It is even more difficult in an environment where lifetime tenure can cause resistance or contribute to a mismatch between the new directions and faculty obsolescence. Even in the best of circumstances, a dean must deal with tenured faculty who procrastinate, complain, behave passively or aggressively, or seek to undermine the new initiatives. A dean must acquire the necessary cross-cultural skills to mediate between the forces of change and the forces of status quo.

Culture of Good Citizenship On and Off Campus

Relationships with fellow academic deans can provide social support, knowledge, experience, and perspective about how other academic units, particularly professional schools, handle issues and problems. Simply knowing how one's fellow deans responded to requests from the provost is informative and insightful. Chairing important university committees and task forces has some obvious merits; such assignments, which often add to an already heavy workload, can provide opportunities to learn more about the university. The knowledge can be an organizational secret or useful gossip about a pending policy change in the university; there also are opportunities for meeting with other university executives, trustees, and important friends and supporters. Access to these sources potentially can benefit one's school and enhance one's authority and respect in the larger university community. Further, there are extended opportunities to conduct school business face-to-face, rather than by bureaucratic memo.

Being a good citizen of the university is critical to successful deaning. One's relationship with the chief academic officer or provost is essential to the management of a school. Mutual respect and maintaining open communications are also important. It is fortunate if the chief academic officer also understands the unique aspects of the social work profession.

The professional school dean must not only give attention to the culture of the university and the professional school, but also must keep abreast of developments and changes in professional practice, other professional schools, and in the larger society. As major stakeholders in professional associations and accreditation organizations, deans must build and maintain relationships with local and national practitioner organizations as well as with politicians at the local, state, and federal levels.

Active participation in the life of the profession is expected, including attending professional meetings, assuming leadership roles, making accreditation site visits, serving on boards of directors, and contributing to the knowledge base of the profession. Professional school deans are expected to be conversant with contemporary social problems, especially with respect to public policies and foundation priorities. Deans often must find their own way on public issues, and evaluate opportunities to speak out on controversial issues.

One's Own Acculturation

At the interface of the relationship between the values of the university and the profession are one's own perspectives, biography, preferences, and values. Over the years as faculty members, deans acquire certain perspectives about the university, professional education, and the role of the profession. Although they bring these viewpoints to the deanship, it is not always clear how to incorporate them into the process of deaning. From the experiences noted in the case studies and the support group processes described in Chapters Three and Four of this volume, it is clear that a dean's personal views, interests, and strengths can become closely linked to the school's goals and directions.

In addition to an awareness of their own interests and capacities, deans must become students of organizational history to gain an understanding of the history, legacies, and past priorities of the school. This approach is even more important for those who took the job as outsiders. Armed with this background knowledge, deans are able to chart new directions and courses of action. Ongoing organizational assessment is needed as new challenges and opportunities present themselves.

The most difficult aspect of deaning is handling one's own feelings. As with any identity issue, knowing who you are, where you have been, and where you want to go are crucial at any stage of the deanship. Upon entering the deanship, the dean begins with his or her own values, ideals, and perspectives. They are tested over time with faculty, students, staff, university administrators, alumni, and others in the professional communities. Some values are challenged, others are reinforced. With so many stakeholders in the life of a professional school dean, it is important to anticipate conflicting and competing expectations, many of which are impossible to address singly or together. One's values and perspectives about administration and human relations must be rock solid. It is also important to note that many of the expectations of a dean are embedded in the institutional role of the deanship and not necessarily related to the dean's personal attributes.

Lessons Learned from Cross-Cultural Experiences

Considering the multiple contexts that require a dean to demonstrate cross-cultural skills, it is clear that guiding organizational change is impossible without an appreciation of the role of culture in organizational life. The faculty and tenure process, the different cultures of the on-campus and off-campus communities, and the dean's own acculturation process require deans to understand the cultures of the systems and audiences with which they interact. At the same time, they need to formulate clear objectives and strategies for change to deal successfully with the many cross-cultural interactions. It is the interaction between organizational culture and the dean's leadership and management roles that has led to the following preliminary set of lessons learned.

Lesson one: maintain a sense of fairness even in the face of conflict. Faculty and staff need to view the dean as a source of trust, good will, and as someone who does not hold a grudge. This lesson is derived from difficult and sometimes painful experience when faculty become frustrated or angry with the dean. In the heat of some disagreement, it is essential to maintain composure; take twenty-four hours to sleep on an issue before reacting or writing a hostile memo. It is also essential to recognize that faculty make a distinction between the dean as person and the dean as role. When they want to complain or express a concern, they usually want to communicate with the dean who is viewed as the individual in charge, not necessarily the unique individual who is in the role of dean. This somewhat fine distinction can take years to fully appreciate.

Lesson two: insist on excellence in all matters. This involves setting standards—from how the school's receptionist handles calls to monitoring the student course evaluations process, to specifying the level of faculty scholarly productivity necessary for promotion.

Lesson three: encourage teamwork and collaboration among faculty and staff. Despite the faculty culture of individualism, there is also a searching for the sense of a scholarly community, whether in the form of colloquia or specially appointed groups to address a particular issue. Support staff need to meet regularly to be kept abreast of changes and emerging issues and to interact with the top administrators of the school. The same is true for internship supervisors, alumni, executives of community organizations, and professional school advisory boards.

Lesson four: demonstrate respect for faculty governance while insisting on administrative prerogatives. The dean is often expected to chair faculty meetings when there is no elected faculty member to carry out this leadership function. The dean usually takes the lead in monitoring faculty assignments to governance committees, being especially concerned about equity so that no faculty member is unduly burdened. At the same time, the dean must understand the prerogatives of academic administration and communicate them to all who are affected.

Lesson five: reward excellence and support for the school's programs. Deans play a key role in judging faculty excellence in teaching, research, and service for annual merit reviews as well as promotions. Excellence includes individual faculty performance and the role individuals play in groups to foster teamwork in addressing the school's mission and priorities. Recognizing and rewarding administrative staff for excellence is equally important in communicating a sense of total community.

Lesson six: seize opportunities to manage conflict and use them as vehicles for organizational change. For many professional school deans, the goal of successful administration is to avoid or reduce conflict. Because conflict is inherent in organizational life, especially academe, where the smallest issue can generate the most heat, deans must learn to manage conflict, not reduce or avoid it. To manage conflict is to channel the energy and heat in the direction of change. This lesson also takes years to fully appreciate and put into practice.

Lesson seven: take time to recuperate away from the school. Taking care of oneself is essential to effective deaning, because no one else will take care of the dean. It is rare and wonderful when the provost makes an unscheduled visit to the dean's office to simply inquire as to how things are going, but deans must find their own ways of reflecting on their progress. Some keep a journal; others take time away from the school to recharge their batteries. Deans often use conferences or out-of-town meetings for this purpose. Others find hobbies that engross them in a world totally different from academe.

Lesson eight: some problems will simply not go away. The most common ones are the need for a bigger budget, insufficient student scholarships, inadequate faculty travel funds, finding high-quality faculty, attracting outstanding students, and improving faculty relations. Although these problems are endemic to professional schools, the measure of success is the progress each dean makes over time in dealing with these challenges.

Reference

Rosovsky, H. "Deaning." *Harvard*, 1987, *89* (3), 34–40.

Richard A. English is dean of the School of Social Work at Howard University, Washington, D.C.

Some have suggested that changing academic institutions is somewhat akin to moving to a graveyard. Others observe that the true test of organizational leadership is the capacity to facilitate change by building on the past and envisioning the future.

Guiding Organizational Change

Michael J. Austin, Frederick L. Ahearn, Richard A. English

The challenge of revitalizing nonprofit organizations can overwhelm staff and administrators (Austin, 1995). The forces of change converge from all directions, from the changes brought on by the information revolution to the constraints caused by having fewer resources. To increase our knowledge of organizational change, this chapter uses three case studies to capture the perceptions of academic administrators. Though the case studies represent retrospective views, the authors were members of a support group that met regularly to share and analyze the information in the case studies. In addition to identifying the similarities and differences found in the three cases, special attention is given to the concepts of organizational culture and the role of administrative leadership.

Each case takes place over a seven-year period, 1985 to 1992. The settings are schools of social work at three major East Coast universities. Each institution has a unique mission: for one it is serving the needs of the Catholic community; for another, serving the needs of the African American community; and for the third, working toward the research priorities found in the Ivy League community. Each of the authors became dean of one of the three schools in 1985 and they shared their learning throughout the process of guiding their respective organizations through change. The social turbulence during this period was significant. Emery and Trist (1965) remind us of the overlooked impact of environmental turbulence on most organizations. The full impact of the Reagan administration cutbacks in social-program spending, as well as the tax cuts of the early 1980s, had hit all three schools by 1985. The slide in enrollments had reached the lowest point in decades. The drastic curtailment of federal and state training grants, along with radically increased competition for research funding, had sent most schools of social work into a fiscal tailspin. It was a period of growing military expenditures and adventures around the globe; rising federal debt; economic chaos in the marketplace, including junk bond mergers and savings and loan bankruptcies; increasing homelessness; rising unemployment and dislocation; overflowing child abuse caseloads; and rapid change at home and around the world.

It was during this period of rapid change that the authors were given the mandate by their university presidents to revitalize their respective schools. The challenge was overwhelming (Austin, 1989). It included finding a way for the schools to respond to the profound changes in the American family and on the streets of U.S. cities; helping faculty respond to the new realities through their teaching and research; responding to student demands for more curricula concerning AIDS, child abuse, sexual assault, homelessness, drug abuse, racism, sexism, and homophobia; revitalizing alumni involvement, with the related pressures to build on the school's strengths and traditions by not changing the school too quickly or radically; and balancing all these pressures with the mandate from higher administration to balance budgets, bring in new sources of funding, and pursue donors to endow student fellowships and professorships.

An Emerging Framework for Case Analysis

Schein (1985) suggests that mature cultures found in organizations with long and rich histories create patterns of perception, thought, and feeling that predispose the organizations to certain kinds of leadership. And, paradoxically, the organizations' leaders not only create cultures, cultures, in turn, create their next generation of leaders. Schein (1985) defines organizational culture as "a pattern of basic assumptions—invented, discovered or developed by a given group as it learns to cope with its problems of external adaptation and internal integration—that has worked well enough to be considered valid and, therefore, to be taught to new members as the correct way to perceive, think, and feel in relation to those problems" (p. 9).

Building on the themes of internal integration and external adaptation, Schein's definition of organizational culture provides a framework for analyzing the three case studies. Internal integration, for this analysis, is the blending of consensus-building and tension-management strategies. Consensus building is fundamental to the academic environment, where people with divergent views struggle to find common ground in an organization that promotes individualism and autonomy. Tension management relates to the organization's interpersonal climate.

In order to stabilize the environment, deans are frequently placed in the position of managing tensions between faculty members, between faculty and staff, between staff and students, and between students. This aspect of internal integration requires the capacity to negotiate differences while continuing to help the organization focus on its mission and goals.

The second component of the framework—external adaptation—is defined in terms of resource acquisition and marketing. Faculty and staff involvement in recruiting outstanding students is a form of resource acquisition because tuition is an essential resource of the school. Similarly, when faculty help secure funded research projects it is like a form of student financial support, considering that research assistantships and overhead cost recovery bring in financial resources, which supply the seed money needed to promote the organization's innovative ventures. The second component of external adaptation involves marketing or community relations. Marketing can lead to recruiting students who might not otherwise apply, alerting providers and funding sources about faculty expertise, and fostering alumni pride in their alma mater (which may lead to increased donations).

Organizational culture—the third component of the framework, beyond internal integration and external adaptation—directly involves the leadership role of the dean. As Schein (1985) notes, in organizations with substantial history, culture becomes a powerful influence on its members. If the culture needs to be changed, it requires leadership at all levels of the organization to "break the tyranny of the old culture" through skillful assessment, unfreezing, redefinition, and change, then refreezing the new assumptions and realities (p. 314). For example, in a school that has a long history of excellence in the education of practitioners and a short history of commitment to research, the cultural changes needed to balance excellence in education and excellence in research can require substantial efforts to unfreeze, change, and refreeze the culture.

While guiding organizational change, deans are called upon to absorb and contain the staff's anxiety, which emerges from the change process or when things go wrong. To meet the staff demand for "temporary stability and emotional reassurance," the dean must maintain continuity with the organization's past while modifying directions to capture opportunities of the future (Schein, 1985, p. 81). Throughout this juggling process, the dean seeks to balance strong competing forces that might run counter to his or her belief system while keeping focused on the vision of a changed organization. Supporters in the organization are essential if the dean is to maintain the organizational vision. While absorbing the tension from above (expectations of central administration), from within (faculty, staff, and students), and from outside (alumni, community leaders, agency executives, and others), deans take on the ethos of the organization. As the following cases reflect, the leadership challenge for the dean is to be able to step outside one's culture while continuing to live within it (Kotter, 1990).

The key aspects of organizational culture for this case study analysis are summarized in the following framework for guiding organizational change: consensus building and tension management (internal integration); resource acquisition and marketing (external adaptation); and absorbing or containing anxiety and promoting a vision (administrative leadership). Given the complexity of guiding organizational change, administrators must be "emotionally strong boundary spanners with high objectivity and tolerance of deviant points of view" (Van Maanen and Schein, 1979). The following three case studies of organizational change are arranged chronologically in terms of beginnings, middles, and endings, or new beginnings.

Case A: New World University

The dean in Case A highlights the internal and external demands on the dean's leadership role as a newcomer to "New World University."

Beginnings. When I decided to accept the offer as dean of the School of Social Work at New World University, my colleagues, friends, and family expressed strong viewpoints. No one was at a loss for words. Opinions generally fell into one of two extremes: that of viewing the move as a great challenge and opportunity made possible by my previous experiences in university administration, and that of considering the move the worst possible decision, one I should have my head examined for.

To alleviate my uncertainty about taking the position, I tried to learn as much as possible about the school and the university. I spoke with many knowledgeable people, and spent an entire week reading faculty meeting minutes and reviewing budget reports, the school's annual reports to the university president, and other documents. I met face-to-face with all faculty members in their offices. In a nearly three-hour meeting with the president and the vice president for academic affairs, my observations and questions were shared and they identified their major concerns about the school: low and declining enrollments, the quality of the student body, the value of continuing the bachelor's in social work (BSW) program, upgrading of the faculty, and the future direction of social work education in the nation.

In the beginning, it seemed that everyone had an opinion about what needed to be done, how to do it, and when. The tasks were enormous, complex, overwhelming. Moreover, few people were willing to take responsibility for the problems or their solutions. The leadership vacuum at the school (the deanship had been vacant for more than three years) meant that many fundamental decisions—appointment of new faculty, student enrollment, the need for new resources, renovations, and physical upkeep—were put on hold. The neglect was omnipresent.

The interior of the modern building had not been painted for years, the elevator frequently broke down, the central air and heating system had never worked properly, many offices were inadequately furnished, furniture was broken, old filing cabinets were empty, and new lockers remained unused. There were no personal computers for students or faculty; the only photocopy machine in the entire school was more than twenty-five years old. Staff and faculty were embarrassed by the poor quality of copies of correspondence sent outside the school, such as grant applications. The old machine became the symbol of the faculty's expectations about my capacity to effect change. When the arrival of the new machine was announced at a faculty meeting after a full year of lobbying central administration, the faculty broke out in applause.

The school's administrative infrastructure also needed serious attention. With the admissions director position vacant, my first endeavor was to become involved in the admissions of new and returning master's degree students, then hire a new admissions director and find the necessary office space. Other critical vacancies included the associate deanship and chair of the doctoral program.

Another pressing task was to complete a self-study for reaccreditation of the master's in social work (MSW) program, which was due eighteen months after my arrival. The school's curriculum had not been brought into line with the new (1983) Council on Social Work Education (CSWE) guidelines, and any changes in the curriculum, policies, or programs required at least one full year of implementation before the Council's accreditation review and site visit. With faculty support, I requested a one-year extension of the visit and placement of the bachelor's and master's programs on the same accreditation cycle.

During my first year, the school's excellent library was being pushed to merge with the central library. To counter that threat, I contacted library colleagues at my former university and asked them to identify any studies that supported branch libraries. Our head librarian also surveyed the eighteen schools of social work that have branch libraries and learned that our library was in the top third in terms of the size of the collection, annual budget, number of full-time professional staff, and acquisitions. The library is still too small, but it was saved from merger.

Other tasks in my first year included planning for the dedication of the social work building to honor the school's first dean, and for the school's golden anniversary. Alumni and community relations had deteriorated, the national alumni organization had become defunct (only a few chapters remained active) and the school's visiting committee had stopped meeting. In addition, although the school enjoyed excellent relations with many public and private community agencies, especially where our graduates were employed in key positions, some of these relationships had fallen into neglect. Yet, the community continued to make demands on the school. Church groups and other voluntary associations frequently asked for technical assistance, help writing grant applications, program evaluations, and student placements.

Everywhere I turned, someone was giving me advice. It was difficult to assess the help offered without the adequate organizational capacity to respond to problems. I was confused, bewildered. During my first Christmas holidays, I retreated into my own thoughts to reevaluate my decision to take the deanship. I realized it was going to be tough, but I decided to stick with it. The complex and competing demands of professional education were aggravated by the scarcity of critical resources and the community's expectation that the school would take leadership and provide service. A strategy for addressing these demands and complex problems began to emerge despite an emotional setback from a chance meeting with the university president during which I asked him when he would be visiting the school. "When you clean up the mess," he responded sternly. Stunned by his reaction, I did not press for further discussion of the matter. Nor did he ever come for a visit.

Middles. The middle years were a period of consolidation. A new associate dean was appointed, and so were the directors of the doctoral program, admissions, recruitment, and financial aid. New faculty members also were brought on board. My feelings of being overwhelmed by problems and demands subsided. A clearer perspective began to emerge about how to guide the school by blending the past with organizational change and development to achieve new goals. My central task during the middle phase was to achieve rapprochement among the various constituent bodies and forge a common vision for the school consistent with its mission as well as its history. The school's curriculum was my top priority.

The creative blending of continuity and change was demonstrated in five substantive areas of curriculum development and renewal. First was development of the overarching conceptual framework of the MSW curriculum. After considerable faculty discussion, six new principles were delineated: (1) making a commitment to public social services, (2) combating societal oppression, (3) recognizing diversity within African American communities, (4) practicing social work with diverse populations, (5) working for social justice, and (6) infusing the program with an international perspective.

The second area of curriculum development and renewal was creation of a new field-of-practice concentration: social work with displaced populations such as refugees, immigrants, migrants, the homeless, and victims of manmade and natural disasters.

The third area involved expansion of the school's commitment to recruit and enroll international students, especially from developing countries. As part of this effort, new overseas field placements were to be developed, articulation agreements with universities abroad negotiated, and external funding sources pursued.

The fourth area of curriculum development was to increase the number of students placed in public social services through a new field practicum unit and securing thirty student stipends.

The fifth area included extensive faculty reassessment of the research curriculum, which resulted in setting up a computer lab and a new course on using computers in human services, and strengthening of the research requirements.

Faculty appointment, promotion, and tenure also became a major area of concern during the middle years. Although new faculty members were hired, some appointments were not renewed. Scrutiny of faculty for tenure and promotion became more rigorous under the new vice president for academic affairs. This created tensions within the school about the potential for successful faculty appointments in the future.

During the middle years we acquired a major unrestricted foundation grant. Most of the funds were invested in a matching endowment for the future development of the school's community-based Family Research and Resource Center. Our equipment budget also grew during the middle years. All secretarial workstations were equipped with computers; laser printers were installed and connected to a local area network system. Work continued on the student computer lab as well as a process for assisting faculty with grant applications and research.

The overall administrative strategy during the middle years included three components: (1) the creative management of scarce resources, (2) the creative blending of continuity and change, and (3) the concerted and continuous pursuit of external funding. Great care was taken in public speeches and daily behavior to explain to faculty, staff, and students how the new ideas and curriculum were bringing change and to emphasize that the innovations were faithful to deeply felt organizational traditions. This approach helped everyone to understand the need for change and to participate in generating new ideas. A new sense of empowerment increased the key constituents' confidence in the school's reputation and contributed to strengthening the academic excellence of programs.

New Beginnings. The new beginnings period was marked by significant institutional change: the resignation of the president of twenty years, along with several other senior administrators; the appointment of an interim president; and the arrival of a new president. The transitional years were filled with expectancy and uncertainty for the whole university.

The changed physical appearance of the school symbolized its new beginnings. Now, paintings of well-known artists grace the walls and an original Alexander Calder tapestry enriches the main lobby. New carpeting dresses up all the common spaces of the building. Two conference rooms are newly furnished. The refurbished student lounge sports new carpeting, furniture, and draperies; additional canteens enhance food and beverage selections. A well-equipped audio-visual lab opened in year six. The student computer lab was completed during the fall term of year seven. The research center is slowly developing, with needed equipment added as funds become available. Each of these accomplishments required persistence and great follow-through.

Student enrollment has increased substantially. Our Five Year Plan's enrollment goal is in sight. It is gratifying that for the first time in almost seven years faculty members are complaining about large classes.

Several new programs have been established and others revitalized. The Cosby Fellowship program for outstanding MSW students was established with a major gift. During the celebration of Social Work Month, a new annual open house program was established: alumni, local practitioners, educators, and agency executives are invited to the school for day-long seminars on practice and social issues. The school's continuing education program was revitalized with a series of courses offered throughout the year for social work practitioners and other human service professionals. A new Early Publications Initiative has had significant results during the past three years. This initiative encourages doctoral students to submit sole-authored publications to refereed journals as a way of giving them a competitive edge upon entering the academic job market. (Six manuscripts have been accepted in the past three years with others under review or being readied for submission.) The strengthening of graduate education and research, the scarcity of resources, and the relatively small enrollment in the baccalaureate program led the faculty to ask the board of trustees to discontinue the program in 1993.

The memory of how things used to be fades even after a short period of seven years. The building looks different; the interpersonal environment is more open and friendlier; new programs have been established and old ones revitalized; enrollment is up; and the overall status of the school has been enhanced. The future course of development for the school has been set: graduate and postgraduate education, research, continuing education, extramural education, and community outreach. The school has already demonstrated that it can attract both private and public financial support and that it can enroll superior graduate students. It is essential that the university provide stable and predictable support for these new beginnings to be successful.

Case B: Sectarian University

The dean in Case B describes the leadership challenges involved in gaining access as a newcomer to the established culture of "Sectarian University."

Beginnings. My decision to seek a deanship was prompted by a personal need for change. After teaching at a northeastern university for seventeen years and managing a social planning and community organization program in the School of Social Work, the work was no longer satisfying. Staying would mean spending another fifteen years waiting to retire; taking a risk would bring a new challenge. When the offer came to take a deanship in another major U.S. city, I accepted it with great anticipation. Not only would it mean returning to my alma mater, it also was a chance to return to an area where there was tremendous political activity and excitement.

When I accepted the offer, the academic vice president made it clear that the school needed to address a number of issues. First among these was the precipitous decline in enrollments, more than 50 percent in the past eight years. A second priority was the need to establish linkages with such audiences as the university at large, alumni, and the local community. Also of great importance to the academic vice president was the necessity to raise the school's standards of research and scholarship.

I was warmly and cordially welcomed by the faculty, students, alums, and community. Many spoke of the proud history of the school; others cited the need for changes. It seemed necessary to understand the past and, at the same time, to capture a vision for the future. Most everyone was ready to consider new paths and there was much support from the administration, faculty, and community.

The culture of the school had been strongly influenced by the tradition of the university with its emphasis on scholarship and research, its commitment to the Catholic Church, and faculty participation in the operation of the university. The School of Social Work faculty was accustomed to discussing not only curriculum policy, but also making recommendations concerning administrative matters.

The school's warm and collegial ambiance was in part due to its modest size, twenty-one faculty members and two hundred fifty full-time students. Although there were differences and disagreements, the social relations within the organization were good. Seventy-one percent of the faculty were relatively young, fairly new to the school, and nontenured. This had both positive and negative aspects. These faculty members were student-oriented, active in practice, prepared to tackle the rigors of research and, for the most part, good teachers. On the other hand, the school did not have a "big name" faculty or an active group of established scholars. The school's culture benefited from the vitality and currency of new ideas brought by the nontenured group. Yet, they expressed concern that they would never meet the stringent requirements for promotion and tenure.

Any new administrator must immediately embark on an assessment of the strengths and weaknesses of his or her organizational system to be able to explore alternative possibilities and remedies in developing a vision of new directions. The participation of relevant constituencies—faculty, students, and alumni—is crucial to achieve consensus. To this end, task forces were set up to define and explore issues such as decline in enrollments, the school's relationship with the community, international programs, and the doctoral program. Every faculty member participated in at least one of these ad hoc groups with the intention of defining the problem, then proposing a range of solutions for a faculty decision.

During the second semester, faculty acted on recommendations to deal with the enrollment problem. Since half of the master's students attended part-time because they had a job or family obligations, late afternoon and evening programs plus a Saturday immersion program were approved. Then, to attract a national audience and increase enrollments, the faculty voted to start a summer MSW program through which a student could complete his or her degree in four summers. Summer sessions also became a popular way for part-time students to accelerate their studies and graduate earlier.

Missing from the enrollment picture was a marketing and recruitment plan. Complicating matters was the fact that the interim director of admissions was a junior faculty member assigned the task for a year or two. It was obvious that the requirements of promotion and tenure (research, teaching, and service) conflicted with the time and skill needed to market, recruit, and administer a very busy office. I decided early to shift resources and the following year hired a full-time administrator (not a faculty member) to manage the admissions office.

Faculty also debated the role of the school in the local community. The school's principal audience traditionally had been the Catholic community nationally. Now, there was more and more concern about the university environs and the community, which was largely African American with a growing population of Latin American refugees. The Urban Affairs Task Force proposed the development of an Institute for Social Justice that would provide technical assistance to neighborhood groups and church-centered agencies working with the homeless, refugees, and other poor; develop financial support to pursue research on oppressed groups and the lack of justice; and create a student unit (fellows of the Institute) to work with faculty on the technical assistance and service.

Five years earlier, with the support of the Fulbright and Interamerican foundations, the school inaugurated a master's of teaching of social work program in Brazil for professors from the sixteen social work schools in the country. Many faculty members had traveled to Brazil to teach in this program and there was a strong commitment to continuing this program and to exploring other international exchanges.

By the end of the first year, the doctoral program task force recommended a dual focus on clinical scholarship and social policy and social justice, both with a strong underpinning of research. A third option for an interdisciplinary program, such as social work and anthropology, also was approved. But before final faculty approval, the proposed program was sent to outside consultants for review. Finally, with the new direction in place, I decided to change the chair of the doctoral program, appointing the person who had chaired the task force and was committed to the changes.

Another thrust was the development of faculty. Two activities were begun by the end of the first year: Portuguese classes and a writers' workshop. Because of the school's commitment to the Brazil program, a number of faculty members wanted private Portuguese classes. A Brazilian professor was hired to provide an intensive course of study for nine faculty members. Although interest was very high at first, it waned in a few months because of the pressures of classes and other activities. Only two faculty members continued with the program.

I arranged for a former editor of *Social Work* to conduct the writers' workshop for a select group of nontenured faculty to enhance their skills in writing for professional journals. Also, a historic black college's School of Social Work was to collaborate with us by sending faculty and financing half the project. The two schools had not worked together much, though they were less than a mile from each other.

Promotion and tenuring of faculty are key moments in a university. Faculty members who have met the requirements of scholarship, teaching, and service, and who are seen as fitting into the goals of the school and the mission of the university sufficiently, receive a contract for life. This School of Social Work had promoted very few of its faculty. Built into the culture of the organization was the belief that this process was controlled by outside individuals and values. Thus, there was considerable pessimism concerning the process as well as one's chances to succeed because it meant approval not only by the school's Committee on Appointments and Tenure (CAP) and the school's faculty, but also by the CAP of the academic senate, the confirming vote of the academic senate, and, in the case of tenure, a vote of the board of trustees Committee on Academic Affairs.

During the first year, as required, two promotion and two tenure cases were presented to the various bodies and, in each case, the request was granted. Each promotion and tenure decision prompted a celebration by the faculty, who saw it as a "victory against the people across the street," referring to the academic senate's CAP, the academic senate itself, and the board of trustees.

By year two, faculty morale was high. They were sharing many activities, and had reached consensus to bring about change. As the new dean, I continued to experience a honeymoon phase throughout the early years. I provided the vision for new directions, encouraged faculty to identify problems and search for solutions, and named key faculty members to manage the implementation of the changes that were voted by the full faculty. The Institute for Social Justice became operative, the evening and summer master's programs were launched, and the changes in the doctoral curriculum were implemented. And, new offices were built, making it possible for every faculty member to have an office.

Hiring new faculty is indeed a means by which a dean can create lasting organizational change. The addition of faculty who support the dean's vision and bring new knowledge and skills to advance the consensus for change is most important. From the beginning, retirements and resignations provided opportunities to add new faculty.

I reached out to the university and local communities to gain visibility, understanding, and support. Within the university, I made the rounds to meet the other administrators, deans, and vice presidents. It was important, especially for the deans, to understand our common problems, to find out about the responsibilities of the various vice presidents, and to learn how to get something done in the bureaucratic environment of the university. Serving on the academic senate oriented me to the faculty's role in university decision making and to the interplay among the schools. Sometime later, I was named chairman of the search committee for a new dean of the Law School and chairman of the academic senate's Committee for Honorary Degrees.

Community relations took the form of visits to agencies and serving on local and national boards of directors. This gave the school visibility as well as opportunities for field placements and to collaborate on grant submissions. I was on the national boards of the National Association of Social Workers (NASW), Catholic Charities USA, the National Center for Social Policy and Practice, and later the National Council on Aging as a way to connect the school with these groups.

As the beginning began to flow into the middle phase, I hired more new faculty members, enrollments stabilized, morale was good, and the school continued to enjoy considerable visibility. Then a renowned priest was denied permission to teach in his area of expertise and a major campuswide controversy ensued. This case lasted several years, raising great concern about academic freedom. A new statement on the subject was formulated, but, unfortunately, a respected scholar was lost.

Middles. The first couple of years were tremendously productive and personally satisfying. The honeymoon seemed endless. Faculty confidence was high and there was a general view that the school was on the move. Everyone was busy; esprit de corps had reached a new high. As dean, I had made a smooth executive entry, developing cordial, if not warm, relationships with the faculty. Relations with the university and the community continued strong, providing the school with much attention and opportunity.

This period coincided with the university's centennial celebration, which allowed the school to plan several successful events. An alumni program awarded five former deans of the social work school the university president's Medal of Honor. A joint program with Catholic Charities USA featured a national figure as speaker who addressed the social and political issues of the day. The Institute for Social Justice collaborated in the planning and implementation of two national conferences on housing for the homeless and one on the mental health needs of refugee children who had been traumatized by war and other violence.

Organizationally, an associate dean had been appointed as well as a new chair of the MSW program. The doctoral program reforms were implemented. Representatives of the Council on Social Work Education visited the school as part of the reaccreditation of the undergraduate program, which was approved without question. The director of field instruction retired, a faculty member resigned, and their replacements were hired. By this time, the admissions office was computerized and all of the administrative assistants were learning to operate their own personal computers.

Because of the university's centennial activities, the School of Social Work was fortunate to receive a $1 million gift to endow a chair for the study of homelessness and issues of social justice. I worked with the development office, meeting potential donors to raise funds for the school. There was much hope that the university could begin its second century on a solid financial footing and schools would have the necessary resources to fulfill their missions.

Though there were notable successes in gaining promotions and tenure, several nontenured faculty members decided not to apply. Instead, they resigned, concluding—accurately—that they had little hope for advancement because they had published little. Whenever this happened, the rest of the nontenured members would feel the repercussions, fearing that the same might happen to them. The dean's role consisted of meeting with faculty members who were considering applying for promotion and tenure; helping them to consider their options if they should decide to resign; and meeting with other faculty members to mitigate the negative effects of a departure.

One particular application for promotion and tenure caused great dismay among the younger ranks. It involved a well-liked and respected woman who was a marvelous teacher and a warm and helpful colleague. Her application was acted on very favorably by the school's CAP and approved unanimously by the faculty only to be turned down by the CAP of the academic senate for deficiencies in research and publications. This decision confirmed many of the old perceptions of the impossibility of promotion and tenure at the university. Many were stunned; others wanted to fight, urging an appeal. I dealt personally with the candidate to address the meaning of the decision and the option of appeal. She filed an appeal and four months later, to the joy of most, was promoted to associate professor and granted tenure.

The international efforts continued. The first class in Brazil graduated, a new cohort was recruited, and classes began again in Rio de Janeiro, with members of the school's faculty traveling twice a year (January and July) to teach. In addition, a joint conference on women's issues in social development was cosponsored with a Philippine School of Social Work. A visit to the Philippines followed.

All came to a sudden end after the associate dean and the chair of the MSW program died within a year of each other. The honeymoon was over; the roof fell in. Both women were loved by all. They were irreplaceable. The faculty felt a tremendous loss and some mourned for several years. Because of the rise of enrollments and the lack of new faculty positions, classes were larger than usual. And with the need to cover the classes of the deceased faculty members, everyone was overburdened. To add to the chaos and tragedy of this time, the new director of field instruction was relieved of her duties because the field operations nearly collapsed. She soon left the school and someone with strong administrative skills was hired.

These losses forced me to focus almost exclusively on internal matters. There were serious organizational problems: the office of field instruction was in shambles, classes were too large, and morale had plummeted. I addressed the faculty's emotional loss through a series of group meetings designed to encourage discussion and personal exchanges. Part-time, adjunct faculty were hired to reduce class size and teaching loads. Major attention was paid to the area of field practica to reestablish sound procedures for selecting agencies, assessing student preference for particular types of placements, and placing students with appropriate field experiences.

During this time, the academic vice president (AVP) resigned. He had been a close friend of our school. He had visited the school to meet faculty; he traveled to Brazil to participate in the social work program there; and he had a very good grasp of the school and its inner workings. His replacement didn't understand the social work profession or the administration of a school as he had never been a dean. New links with the university administration had to be developed. This was particularly a challenge since the new AVP defined his role as the implementor of the executive vice president's plans rather than as an advocate for the deans. Trouble loomed on the horizon.

Near the end of the fourth year, I announced that I intended to seek another four-year term. Several tenured faculty members used this opportunity to insist that the dean present a plan for the future. They made it clear that they might not support me for another term. My accomplishments were not discussed. Faculty seized the opportunity to tell the university's administration they felt overworked. Administrators asked them who they wanted to be dean. The unpleasant process reflected the ennui of the faculty. In the end, they voted overwhelmingly for me to continue as dean.

It was two years before the school regained organizational balance. As new faculty members were hired, the pressure of workloads diminished and the size of classes returned to normal. Slowly, faculty cohesiveness and morale were reasserted. The organization had changed. There was no longer an associate dean position as resources had been diverted to strengthen the office of field instruction. After two MSW chairs in two years, a permanent replacement was appointed, adding to program stability. It was time to think about reaccreditation.

Endings and New Beginnings. There comes a time when a dean must ask himself or herself, How long am I going to continue in this position? Implicit in the question is, How long can one be effective continuing to implement the vision one began with as well as regularly reappraising the school's goals and vision? There is always the danger that one reaches the limits of what can be accomplished and it may be time to move on. We all have examples of outstanding administrators who stayed too long and, unfortunately, are remembered not by their successful accomplishments, but by their inability to govern and their failures. There comes a time to take stock of one's own personal accomplishments and goals as well as the needs of the school at a particular moment. Does one stay, or is it time to do something else?

This process of reassessment was highlighted by two things. First, the second four-year term would soon come to an end and I needed to inform the administration and faculty if I intended to seek another term. And, second, I needed to appraise my plans for the future. What would be best for me? What would be in the best interests of the school?

After seven years, there had been a number of accomplishments. There had also been disappointments, failures, and some unfinished business. The accomplishments included stabilizing enrollments. From a 50 percent decline in admissions to the school, inquiries, applications, and enrollments grew rapidly until it was decided to stabilize the number of students in line with faculty resources and available space. This decision was also prompted by the desire for smaller classes. By the 1991–92 academic year, the school was graduating about ten DSWs, one hundred ten MSWs, and fifteen BA students. The average age of the MSW students had increased to thirty-five (reflecting a process of career changes), and their Miller Analogy Test (MAT) mean score was sixty, about 20 percent above the national average for social work.

Another accomplishment was the recruitment of a dynamic, diverse faculty who proved to be capable of doing scholarly research as well as developing into fine, competent teachers. I got to recruit more than half of the faculty, all at the assistant professor, nontenured level. Minority representation on the faculty changed from 9.5 percent in the 1985–86 academic year to 22.6 percent in 1991–92.

The hiring of faculty also can lead to disappointments. A few promising faculty members experience difficulties and do not develop as planned. A major hurdle for them is the production of research and the publication of scholarly work. Some lack teaching skills or are unable to fit snugly into the school's environment. In any case, it raises the question of what a dean must build into the system to support young, nontenured faculty so they can be promoted and receive tenure. As more women are hired, there must be greater sensitivity to such issues as day care, work schedules, and maternity leave. Among the big disappointments for deans is the realization that a promising faculty member will not make it in academia.

Another accomplishment during this period of reassessment was the strengthening of the school's international focus. The master's program in Brazil graduated two classes of social work teachers, five of whom are deans among the sixteen schools of social work in that country. A new class is now being recruited. Informal educational exchanges have been developed with a School of Social Work in the Philippines and with an association of social educators in the former Soviet Union. In both instances, there have been faculty exchanges and discussion of joint research projects.

The development of the Institute for Social Justice had a number of unanticipated consequences. In the beginning, the school went all out to help small community groups plan, organize, and manage their programs. However, in later years, faculty found the supervision of students to be time-consuming and burdensome. Efforts to attract research in areas of justice and the consequences of oppression never materialized. On the positive side was the development of the theme of social justice and its incorporation into new course offerings at both the MSW (required) and DSW (elective) levels. However, it became evident that the Institute for Social Justice needed to be reassessed.

During this period, the greatest failure was the inability of the school to attract new resources, either from the university or outside sources. Even though the school enlarged and then stabilized enrollments, the additional students did not translate into additional faculty positions. In fact, the school's budget was cut as the tuition-dependent university experienced a decline in undergraduate enrollment. The school must soon decide if it can continue to do all that it does with limited support from the university.

The quest for outside funding for scholarships and research has been disappointing. Since 1985, the school's scholarship grants from the National Institute of Mental Health and the Department of Health and Human Services expired and only one new grant proposal was successful, the Patricia Roberts Harris Fellowship Program to recruit minorities for leadership positions in the public sector. During the same period, several research proposals were written, resulting in modest funds for research. The faculty had excuses, including the heavy workload, for not having time to respond to research proposals.

For three and a half years, our school and a neighboring School of Social Work together pursued the funding of a Title IV-E child welfare training center. A number of factors intervened to block this effort, including the death of the commissioner of social services and the mayor's political and legal difficulties. Now, with new political leadership, the proposal is again alive. Both schools struggle with how to structure a collaboration that is indeed equal and just and also capable of providing for the training needs of the child welfare staff in the area.

Another accomplishment was the planning and implementation of national conferences on homelessness and refugee children. Both conferences pulled together practitioners and researchers to consider theories, research, and services for those populations. And, because of its location and interest in international social work, our school collaborated with the 1992 World Assembly.

While I was taking stock of accomplishments and unfinished business, the usual issues of recruitment, promotion, tenure, admissions, curriculum review, alumni, community service, university committees, and service continued. Two processes were notably significant: the reaccreditation of the BA program in Social Work and the MSW program, and a contentious promotion and tenure hearing. The reaccreditation process lasted about two years and involved the faculty in retreats, meetings, and small group discussions of the mission and goals of the school and the nature of its curricula for the 1990s. Interestingly, this increased faculty morale, giving all a sense of purpose and direction. In contrast, the promotion and tenure issue divided the faculty. It involved a faculty member who had been with the school for thirteen years and was generally regarded as one of our best teachers. However, faculty opinion differed with regard to her scholarship and collegiality. The case is now on appeal and faculty members still differ about whether this person merits promotion and tenure.

As I consider my options for the future, a number of things remain to be done that would be on the agenda for a new—or continuing—dean. Perhaps most important is for the school to put its ambitious goals into balance with its limited resources. Given the university's financial condition, the school is not likely to receive additional funds. Therefore, whoever is dean must lead the school's constituencies in considering whether to reduce the size of the student body, offer fewer elective courses, increase class size, or even drop the undergraduate program. Should the school be downsized?

Now, with reaccreditation over and the curriculum in excellent shape, it is imperative to address the needs of nontenured faculty, to identify barriers to promotion and tenure, and to build into the system the supports necessary for faculty members to become productive scholars, competent teachers, and engaged in service to the school, the university, and the professional and local communities. The school's talented and diverse nontenured faculty enrich the school by their activities. Unfortunately, these faculty members are, at times, pessimistic about their future at the school.

Another future goal is in the area of alumni relations. I have had limited success in developing a cohesive and broadly based association of graduates. Such an organization could help the school raise money for scholarships, locate new field placements, and get individuals to return to the school to lecture, run workshops, and so forth. The school does have an effective newsletter that is published twice a year, but little else.

Given the university's emphasis on research and the needs of its doctoral program, the School of Social Work needs to be involved in a variety of research projects that generate new knowledge as well as test strategies and interventions for innovative practice. Two concerns are evident. First, to get enough resources to implement basic and applied research projects; second, to motivate the faculty to become more involved in investigations and studies that advance the practice of social work.

As my second term draws to a close, I consider what I've accomplished as well as what remains to be done. I have seriously considered taking a high-level government position, another administrative post in academia, a directorship of a social service agency, or returning to teaching. After much thought, I rejected these options and decided to ask for another four-year term to complete the agenda that was set in 1985 and to address the new issues the school faces in the 1990s.

I entered my eighth year confident about my decision to seek another term. The school was generally in good shape despite problems with personnel and budget. The key item on the agenda for the year was to reorganize the school's administrative structure. I didn't realize how many things were about to go very wrong.

The first big problem to resolve was the contested tenure case. The faculty was split over the candidate's research qualifications and, though she had received a tie vote at the school level, her application was voted down by the academic senate. The candidate hired an attorney to appeal the negative decision. As the process grew increasingly litigious, several faculty members wrote to the AVP in support of the candidate. They accused other faculty members of bias against her. Feelings ran high and faculty members became antagonistic. In the end, the university trustees granted the person tenure.

Another problem arose when I proposed hiring a distinguished faculty member from another university. The same forces that fought for tenure for the faculty member just mentioned decided to attack my recommendation. They used delaying tactics at meetings, hallway gossip, and letters to the AVP to discredit the nomination. Despite these efforts by three faculty members, the faculty overwhelmingly approved the appointment, which subsequently was passed by the academic senate and the board of trustees.

As the eighth year ended, I seriously considered resigning. I felt hurt, angry, disgusted, and generally fatigued. Was it all worth it? Obviously, some people could be destructive without knowing the harm they were causing others and the school. In general, the faculty was deeply divided. The majority (eighteen) rallied around me for reappointment as dean; the unhappy four became increasingly isolated.

After much anguish, thought, and consultation I decided to stay on for two more years, then step down as dean. This would allow me to protect those who supported me, announce my resignation with plenty of time to find a replacement, and have enough time to plan a sabbatical and think about the next steps. Once this unannounced decision was made, I felt immediate relief.

Now that the ninth year has begun, the focus has been on celebrating the school's seventy-fifth anniversary. I had organized eleven task forces of faculty, alums, and students to plan a series of celebratory events. The kickoff dinner was a huge success. The president of the university honored four alumni with the presidential medal. More than two hundred enjoyed the festivities. Other events included scholarly presentations on a host of topics: ethics, homelessness, health care, refugees, the future of the profession, and the future of the school. At each event, alumni with distinguished careers were honored.

I also had spent many hours with the development office organizing a fundraising campaign with the goal of raising $750,000. The campaign consisted of asking faculty to pledge, writing alums and following up with a phonathon, writing proposals for government grants to fund specific projects, and approaching foundations to help finance the school's goals.

The atmosphere has improved dramatically since last year. All have rallied around the seventy-fifth anniversary activities even though the split among the faculty will likely remain for a very long time. The faculty all collaborated on the planning and implementation of the anniversary events and together set specific goals for research and developed concept papers for discussion and potential funding.

At the end of my ninth year I announced my resignation effective at the end of my tenth year. Who will succeed me? It depends whether the president decides to bring in an outsider—someone who may be able to bring the two faculty factions together—or an insider who knows and understands the school, its problems, and its actors.

Meanwhile, the school continues to function well. Enrollments are up, the faculty is busy with the anniversary activities, and a number of new grants have been awarded to the school as a result of faculty initiatives. It is amazing that an atmosphere can change so rapidly.

Case C: Ivy University

The dean in Case C reflects on the challenges rooted in mobilizing the professional school community as a newcomer to "Ivy University."

Beginnings. Recruiting a dean is like two apprehensive partners dancing. The partners are the prospective dean and the provost. With the acceptance of the deanship comes the marching orders. At Ivy University, the School of Social Work needed to correct the imbalance between professional education and research. The school was part of a research university, so research needed a higher profile. In addition, the marching orders included such goals as balancing the budget, improving faculty and staff morale, and helping to set the school's direction. Although the provost understood these challenges, the entering dean could only see the tip of the iceberg and needed firsthand experience to assess what lay below the water line in terms of the school's strengths and areas for improvement.

Entering the School of Social Work required me, as the new dean, to develop a strategy for confronting realities and guiding organizational change. The many items of unfinished business on the dean's agenda at times appeared overwhelming. The reaccreditation team's visit six months after I arrived was compounded by the fact that the traditional self-study report had not been completed. In addition, four tenure review cases were scheduled for the spring and most proved to be difficult cases. The faculty's morale was very low, in part because of the archaic governance structure that did not distribute the governance workload equitably. In addition, all Ivy University schools were expected to develop a five-year plan for the provost's review, but the planning process had not started. The building and equipment were in disrepair (air conditioning was broken, telephone system was archaic, aged photocopy machine, broken furniture, and so forth) and needed immediate attention. MSW program enrollments had declined steadily from 1980–85 with no end in sight. As a result, the school was operating at a budget deficit and the administration was putting on the pressure to reduce expenditures, especially to close the branch library.

I had come from outside the school and the region. My first assignment was to learn the university's processes and the norms of the school. It was important to understand the school's history and its educational philosophy, which had emerged over seventy-five years. At the same time, I needed consultants to help me deal with the many demands. The first consultant helped me draft the five-year plan that was to be reviewed by all of the key constituencies at the end of year one. The plan gave me my first opportunity to identify the key environmental factors that impact the school and identify new initiatives, such as social work in the workplace and linking the school with public child welfare agencies. At the same time, a second consultant's help was key to the satisfactory completion of the reaccreditation team's site review. A third consultant was hired to develop and implement a student recruitment program. A fourth consultant helped to revise our student recruitment materials, and a fifth consultant provided editorial assistance as the school developed its statement of educational philosophy. A sixth consultant, from the central campus library, helped assess the viability of the school's branch library. Outside assistance was needed because of the heavy demands already placed on staff and faculty.

In this beginning phase, it was necessary to build relationships with faculty, staff, and students. With the faculty, it was important that I identify those with leadership potential as well as determine future faculty needs. With administrative staff, some staff functions had to be reorganized and new staff, including a new development officer, oriented. I sought out faculty members who had a clear memory of the school's recent history and those who were optimistic about a future that involved innovation and change.

Students and alumni added items to the dean's agenda. Student task forces advocated for curriculum and program changes, and demanded that the school put its educational philosophy in writing. The alumni worried that the new dean might radically change the curriculum and lose the unique educational approach they had experienced. Some of the alums' concerns were allayed when an administrative staff member was designated to help establish an active alumni association.

The school's relationship to the community also needed strengthening. The community advisory board did not have enough corporate representatives, so eight new members were recruited to help develop a fundraising and community-relations strategy. Outreach to nonprofits, foundations, and government agencies was combined with service on key nonprofit boards of directors. Given the challenges facing the school, it was clear that it needed greater visibility on campus and in the community.

The transition from the beginning to the middle phase was marked by my growing confidence and control over my calendar. Early on, the calendar filled up without my knowing whom to see personally and whom to refer to someone else. Exploratory meetings with key people on and off campus helped me determine who was in a position to help the school. The end of the beginning phase was marked by greater confidence in reading the environment, knowing which issues were critical, and understanding the cyclical nature of problems as they emerge during an academic year. What might have been resolved on the "first pass" could return again in a different form but with no less urgency.

Middles. After the frenetic pace of the first eighteen to twenty-four months, the demands of the beginning phase evolved into the slower, more demanding relationship-building activities of the middle phase. The slow, steady process of building faculty confidence in the new leadership was combined with the development of new directions for the school. Foundation funding was secured for a research center to address workplace issues, along with contracts to train public child welfare agency staff.

New faculty were recruited to enhance the school's research and education capacity. As junior faculty members arrived and senior faculty retired, it became clear that the middle phase involved managing transitions of entry, exit, and continuity. University relations needed that same intensity of relationship building to enhance the school's profile. New dual-degree programs and a restructured Ph.D. program took several years to develop and negotiate through a system reluctant to change. Similar ventures were made with other higher education institutions to develop community linkages that could result in dual-degree and certificate programs.

A second wave of consultants was hired to assess the administrative support systems and design a policies and procedures manual; upgrade the computerized information system in the areas of recruitment, admissions, financial aid, and student field placements; and assess the school's research mission. Consultation was also sought to further upgrade materials used for student recruitment and alumni relations. These efforts led to the hiring of a communications consultant to develop a plan for reaching prospective donors and the wider community.

The biggest challenge during the middle phase was to involve senior faculty in the mentoring of junior faculty and help them develop a program of research. This challenge included confronting long-standing school norms. The school historically had primarily provided a sound educational program to prepare MSW practitioners, so to introduce an equal commitment to research and knowledge development was difficult. The research orientation of the doctoral program had been tolerated but not integrated into the central norms of the school. In addition, new faculty who arrived with a research orientation directly challenged the norms of the old guard. The resulting tensions were manifest in curriculum meetings, faculty meetings, student town hall meetings, and faculty workload conferences. This tension spilled over into the important area of grant writing. Senior faculty wrote very few grant proposals and junior faculty were expected to write grants, so it became apparent that recognition of the fundraising effort would create new tensions over salary increases and issues of equity. The raises were related to excellence in teaching, scholarly productivity and research grant activity, and community services. In the past, teaching and community service had been the primary criteria. An excellence in teaching award was established with public recognition given at graduation, listing of faculty names on a special plaque, and faculty salary recognition.

At the same time, faculty and staff were being equipped with new personal computers, and a computer lab was created for students. Student enrollments were increasing because we aggressively recruited students in other regions of the country. The budget was balanced for the first time in nearly a decade, and faculty and staff morale was improving steadily. Support staff competencies improved with the hiring of new staff, and administrative services were coordinated more effectively. An administrative team began to emerge.

For several years, a small group of faculty members worked to recast the school's nationally recognized educational philosophy into a brochure that was sent to alumni and applicants. The statement also helped new faculty to understand the contemporary relevance and vitality of the evolving philosophy. A new forward momentum had been generated, and members of the school community were engaged productively in improving all aspects of the school.

Endings and New Beginnings

The foundation was laid for building upon the school's rich history as it planned for its future. After seven years, a new self-study was well under way in advance of a site team visit. The five-year planning process began with more thorough bottom-up involvement from the faculty than the hurried top-down approach of five years earlier.

The tangible aspects of the seven-year legacy included doubled enrollments and better quality of applicants, doubled alumni donations, and increased classroom space in the building. Many new programs were launched: part-time MSW, continuing education, three certificate programs, five dual-degree programs, and a workplace research program. A development plan was completed, half the faculty was new, and the school's scholarly record quadrupled. The substantial change in the composition of the faculty offered an opportunity to recruit more women to create gender balance (fifty-fifty) and to hire faculty with research competence and practice experience.

Somehow it is easier to list the tangible aspects of a dean's legacy than the intangible, which are related to visibility, morale, sense of direction, and teamwork. All are difficult to measure, so progress must be assessed in small steps. Visibility improved through better signage on the school's building, media attention on and off campus, requests for expert opinions, invitations to participate in agency and interagency activities, and printed materials used to continuously share news about the school.

Faculty and staff morale improved as a greater sense of participation and responsibility emerged, with faculty leaders developing issue papers on key themes, expanding their involvement in campus faculty governance, presenting papers at conferences, and actively using the revised governance structure. There was a growing sense among the faculty that excellence in instruction could be balanced with excellence in scholarship. Colleagues were collaborating more on research and with faculty outside the school.

The administrative and support staff also displayed a greater sense of teamwork. Their roles and functions had been clarified and documented in an administrative policies and procedures manual. Also, computerization led to greater coordination between the needs of administrators and the data management responsibilities of support staff. Staff reported a new sense of commitment—they took more pleasure in coming to work, collaborated with others, felt supported by the dean, and wanted to continuously improve the school's administrative systems.

Identifying the unfinished business of the school was also important. A tuition-driven school's biggest challenge is to expand the funding, restricted and unrestricted. The fundraising plan was designed to raise $10 million to endow student scholarship, faculty chairs, and research centers. Prospecting for major donors will be on the school's agenda for the foreseeable future. Fundraising requires continuing efforts to enhance the school's visibility through local, regional, and national media. This also will help to increase donor recognition of the school's contributions.

The second major challenge is to complete the school's next five-year plan. The plan needs to reflect new and innovative curricular directions as well as ways to fund faculty research projects. Innovative curricula could include internationalizing all the courses as well as unlocking the gridlock of elective options (students can choose only two electives out of sixteen courses). As senior faculty retire, the new dean will be able to recruit new research-competent faculty.

The third major challenge is to keep all of the school's initiatives moving ahead on schedule while upgrading faculty through grant-funded research and innovative instruction. Key to this strategy will be collaborative arrangements with faculty outside the school and improved ongoing mentoring of junior faculty.

Conclusion

Some preliminary conclusions and lessons are drawn from the three brief case studies based on the identification of similarities and differences between the cases, and the organizational culture themes of internal integration, external adaptation, and administrative leadership are used to speculate on some lessons learned.

Similarities and Differences. The case studies are only capsule summaries of a seven-year adventure. Many details have been left on the cutting-room floor: stories too painful to share, issues too controversial to put in print, frustrations with university administration too sensitive to reveal, or stresses too numerous to recount.

On the positive side are successful fundraising efforts, appreciation from faculty and staff, and other public acknowledgments. A major limitation of this case study approach is that it fails to take into account the perceptions of faculty, staff, and central administration. However, numerous similarities and differences in the cases warrant analysis and cautious generalization.

The similarities reflected in the three cases should be apparent. In each case the dean was selected after a national search and arrived at a private university as an outsider and successor to a long-serving predecessor. All three schools were in financial disarray with declining enrollments and low faculty morale, yet each dean was able to reverse the direction of these key indicators of organizational vitality. In each case the dean had to understand the school's unique historical legacy and philosophy and promote a vision of the school's future. There were curricular problems to deal with and the functioning of administrative staff needed to be improved in each case. Long-deferred equipment and building improvement decisions needed immediate attention. Some faculty and staff members needed to be terminated, others deserved to be recognized and promoted. All three schools needed a better relationship with central administration and with constituencies in the community. Each dean had to contend with administrative personnel changes. In all three cases, the dean was given similar marching orders—to address the critical problems and take the school in new directions, especially in relationship to the university's research mission.

Upon arrival, each dean engaged in a complex assessment process. One dean had done extensive homework before accepting the position, the other two did their homework after arrival. The cognitive and interpersonal processes used in the assessment included analyzing national trends and projections, using consultants and colleagues for advice, developing faculty task forces, involving advisory boards of lay leaders and alums, gathering advice from other deans, and actively participating in a dean's support group (described in Chapter Four of this volume). The assessments included determining what was worth preserving and what needed changing. As an outsider, each dean had to assess the nature of the fit between the organization's patterns of workflow and his own management style. It became important to determine quickly which fights to join and which to ignore.

The assessment phase also directly affected each dean's level of expectations. In some cases, the problems were so substantial that they took longer to solve than expected. Each dean had to find ways to connect his own emerging expectations with the expectations of central administration, the community (agency staff and school alums), and the faculty and staff. Early on, each dean was forced to reassess his original expectations, which had served as motivation to accept the deanship. Much soul-searching took place. It became clear that, because expectations are linked to the degree of support, the entry phase represented a time of continuous probing, on and off the campus, to assess the potential for financial and political support. It also became obvious that ongoing reassessment was necessary to guide the organizational change.

The issue of personal values emerged repeatedly during the entry phase. Each dean valued the importance of applied action research, in which faculty and students jointly explore key social welfare issues locally, nationally, and internationally. Each dean came from a setting where faculty governance was active and effective and so wanted that in his newly adopted school. Similarly, there was a deep commitment on the part of all three deans to recognize and support faculty prerogatives while asserting administrative prerogatives. The most obvious administrative prerogatives were to balance the budget, promote curriculum development and renewal, realign the administrative system, foster faculty development, and articulate an organizational vision for all constituencies to review and refine.

The differences among the three cases are also important. Each school had a different historical legacy and educational philosophy. The faculties differed substantially in terms of race, gender, age, tenure, and research competence. The deans came from different academic backgrounds and regions of the country. The life cycle of the organizational change process also differed in each school. In one case, the honeymoon period was longer than the others. Two of the deans had greater success fostering collaboration in the community than the third.

Organizational Cultures. In analyzing the three cases, several cross-cutting themes related to organizational culture emerge. The analytical framework noted earlier can now be used to understand organizational change in relationship to key aspects of organizational culture. The key aspects included internal integration (consensus building and tension management), external adaptation (resource acquisition and marketing), and administrative leadership (absorbing and containing anxiety and promoting a vision).

The first theme related to organizational culture involves the administrative leadership required to promote a vision of the school's future while containing faculty and staff anxiety about change. It required considerable administrative effort to overcome faculty and staff preoccupation with the past in order for them to think about the future. Contemplating the future required recognition of each school's rich history as a foundation for planned change. In each case, it was necessary to articulate and reaffirm the school's educational philosophy (for example, social work practice, commitment to the African American community, or religion in relation to social justice). If the school's programs and directions were not clear to all parties, it would be difficult to address the issue of declining enrollment and fundraising.

The themes of internal integration (consensus building and tension management) and external adaptation (resource acquisition and marketing) represent powerful forces affecting organizational change. The efforts to harness these forces follow, in the form of lessons for guiding the change process.

Consensus building and tension management (internal integration)
1. The dean must assume multiple roles with respect to internal affairs (problem solving, mediating, assessing the sources of conflict resolution, clarifying values).
2. As an organizational culture evolves, it must be reassessed regularly, because new faculty and staff affect the perceptions, feelings, and actions of the group.
3. Consensus about the school's mission needs to be reassessed regularly (more frequently than the eight year intervals required for reaccreditation).

Resource acquisition and marketing (external adaptation)
4. Advocating for resources requires considerable personal investment and energy as well as continuously refining resource acquisition skills (relationship building with donors and foundations, identifying resources for faculty research, maximizing the contributions of university development staff, and continuously making a case to central administration for the school's fiscal needs).
5. Managing the external relations of a school involves the regular collection of perceptions and feedback as well as a distinctly proactive posture with respect to relations with the profession, the community, and the university community.
6. Continuous vigilance of those who claim to support the school to assess any slippage that may threaten the survival of programs or the school itself.

Research is needed to determine whether the case experiences and analyses are similar to those in different settings. For example, are the issues different for deans in public universities? Are there significant differences for deans who are promoted from within? Or for women deans? Or for deans whose tenure exceeds ten years? These and other questions could guide future research.

References

Austin, M. J. "Executive Entry: Multiple Perspectives on the Process of Muddling Through." *Administration in Social Work,* 1989, *13* (4), 55–71.

Austin, M. J. "Using TQM Principles in Child Welfare Organizations." In B. Gummer and P. McCallion (eds.), *Total Quality Management in the Social Services: Theory and Practice.* Albany, N.Y.: Rockefeller College, State University of New York, 1995.

Emery, F. E., and Trist, E. L. "The Causal Texture of Organizational Environments." *Human Relations,* 1965, *18,* 21–32.

Kotter, J. P. "What Leaders Really Do." *Harvard Business Review,* 1990, *68* (3), 103–111.

Schein, E. H. *Organizational Culture and Leadership.* San Francisco: Jossey-Bass, 1985.

Van Maanen, J., and Schein, E. H. "Toward a Theory of Organizational Socialization." In B. M. Stan and L. L Cummings (eds.), *Research in Organizational Behavior.* Vol. 1. Greenwich, Conn.: JAI Press, 1979.

MICHAEL J. AUSTIN *is professor in the School of Social Welfare at the University of California, Berkeley and dean emeritus of the School of Social Work at the University of Pennsylvania.*

FREDERICK L. AHEARN *is professor and dean emeritus at the National School of Social Services, Catholic University of America, Washington, D.C.*

RICHARD A. ENGLISH *is dean of the School of Social Work at Howard University, Washington, D.C.*

It can be lonely at the top or near the top. Finding understanding colleagues who can appreciate your dilemmas and provide relevant feedback is essential for successful deaning.

The Peer Support Group Needed to Guide Organizational Change Processes

Michael J. Austin

The tasks and activities described in the three case studies discussed in Chapter Three do not always reflect the stress or the exhilaration experienced by each dean seeking to guide organizational change in his school. This chapter explores some of the behind-the-scenes issues. The vehicle for identifying and assessing the emotional demands on deans involved in organizational change was a peer support group composed of the three deans.

The idea for the group took hold following informal conversations at a 1986 national meeting of social work deans where the three members discovered that they were in their first year as dean. For seven years, the trio met quarterly for day-long sessions, rotating from one school to another. As with most support groups, the agenda for each session grew out of each dean's current trials and tribulations. Over the years the topics included handling your first tenure or promotion case, selecting an associate dean and other senior administrators, fostering alumni leadership, dealing with contentious faculty members, stanching the flow of red ink in the budgetary process, fostering a climate of responsiveness to student concerns, dealing with administrators, and finding time to think about future directions. None of us had had sufficient prior contact with successful role models who might have helped guide us as advisers or been our mentors.

Beginning

Each case study was constructed with a beginning, middle, and end. The peer support group was structured the same way. In the beginning, we struggled with many questions and gave ourselves permission to take the time to explore them. Following is a sampler of the questions raised and a brief discussion of each.

- Where is the profession headed by the year 2000?
- How do you acquire a quick but thorough understanding of the school's organizational culture?
- How do you develop a vision of the school's future and build support for it?
- How do you understand and manage the stress of entering a senior management position?
- How do we develop sufficient trust among ourselves to share confidential issues with ease? (This last question was unstated.)

Excited and filled with the anticipation of new beginnings, we discussed the future of the profession over several hours-long sessions. Surprisingly, there was consensus on the potential for change despite the Reagan White House's antisocial welfare comments and the conservative academics arguing that social workers were contributing to the growth of social problems. Each of us knew that our school had to identify areas of social work practice that represented cutting-edge issues and that would grow in importance into the next century. Those issues included social justice at the neighborhood level as well as in the developing world; displaced populations, including the homeless, refugees, and immigrants; and workplace issues affecting the working poor as well as the middle class. These themes were then developed into research and training programs by adding onto a school, in whole or in part. The other social welfare themes we discussed were the changing demographic trends related to the young and the old, the changing family, changes in the employment structure, and the changes in the financing of human services. Our shared goal was to speculate on the year 2000 and how our schools would have to respond to the new requirements for practice and the type of faculty that would be needed to be on the cutting edge of change.

We also sought to understand our schools' organizational culture (annual rituals, meeting norms, special terms and language, traditional behaviors). This proved to be a challenging experience for all of us. Typically, tenured faculty members are the carriers of perceptions and traditions that evolve over time. If they acted as elder statesmen and stateswomen by assuming leadership roles and facilitating the inclusion of nontenured faculty, new students and the new dean, then the acquiring of an understanding of the schools' culture was greatly enhanced. However, such leadership was rare. As a result, each of us had to pursue historical information inside and outside the school. One example of senior faculty support was the guidance that came from one faculty member in the form of a year-long tutorial on the history of the school's social work practice philosophy. This collaboration resulted in publishing the school's philosophy and distributing it to prospective students and alumni. Needless to say, acquiring an understanding of a school's traditions and philosophy was not easy for any of us.

Another area our support group discussed extensively was the pressure from central university administration for each school to develop strategic plans that would chart the school's future and provide a context for budgetary decisions. The planning process also was needed to address several years of enrollments declining nationwide during the early 1980s and the resulting budget deficits or constraints. Our support group proved valuable as a forum for sharing, consulting, and relieving the tension surrounding the substantial budgetary pressures. In addition to giving voice to great anxiety and stress, we shared extensively information about federal grant opportunities, potential foundation sources, and state and federal student stipend support. Budgetary themes recurred throughout the support group process as we struggled to gain university resources for faculty, equipment, facilities, and students. One dean fought for four years to get money from central administration to build more classrooms in the school. Another dean fought to preserve his school's budget from central administration's repeated attempts to cut back. The third dean had to advocate for a salary increase after five years of meager or no increases. In all three cases, considerable effort and frustration were expended to gain control over the schools' budgetary process, which had been allowed to drift for years.

During the first few years, our support group discussions would frequently return to sharing our frustrations, successes, and disappointments. Although we enjoyed sharing our small accomplishments and victories along the way, we also struggled to share our reactions to the personal exhaustion emerging from a dean's daily challenges. This process was somewhat compounded by our limited experience in talking about ourselves in a group. Our family backgrounds (Irish American, African American, and German-Jewish American) did not prepare us sufficiently for such open and honest sharing of feelings and anxieties with men in a group. We wondered out loud whether we had taken the wrong job, were about to experience a major professional failure, or whether we could control our tempers in hostile situations. Our many hours of sharing resulted in a powerful bonding.

And, finally, when our support group began, the process included an unstated question: Could we trust each other with confidential and personal information? As we each took greater and greater risks in sharing our worries, this issue became less and less important. We told each other about our visits to the doctor for stomach ailments, stress-induced sleeplessness, balancing the demands of home and spouse with the job demands, intense feelings generated by interacting with people who repeatedly challenged and undermined our efforts to provide guidance during times of organizational crisis. One member of our group kept a journal in which he could "park" the frustrations of guiding organizational change.

Middles

As we settled into the middle phase that followed two to three years of entry and adjustment, new questions emerged. Following are some examples.

- How do we deal with contentious faculty members?
- How do we handle relations with central administration?
- How do we build teamwork among our administrative staff?
- How do we foster effective alumni and student relations?
- How do we handle the reaccreditation process?
- How do we promote effective teaching?

Most deans search for ways to foster open and direct communications with faculty. Through individual conferences, group committee meetings, and faculty meetings, deans explore areas of shared understandings and common ground for consensus building. This exploration is frequently hampered by contentious faculty members who fail to use office procedures. This results in support staff frustration and tension, sabotaged program initiatives, or refusal to be accountable for administrative responsibilities. Although the vast majority of faculty-dean interactions were productive and cordial, the persistent minority of contentious interactions could try the patience of the most skillful academic administrator.

The support group discussions also focused on relations with central administration. After two to three years of budget presentations, it became clear that dealing with a provost or academic vice president can be challenging. Many hours of discussion were devoted to exploring different strategies for advocating for more university resources devoted to the school's initiatives. At times, for some, budget presentations were quite tense as requests were systematically refused. At other times, persistent requests were ultimately approved after years of advocacy.

In addition to the budget process, we were pressed to advocate for other issues as well. These included faculty promotion applications and new appointments, support from other areas of university administration, and for recognition of one's own role as dean. For example, one dean finally had to confront central administration with the fact that his low salary was out of line with comparable schools. Another dean had to confront the provost for not being supportive during senior management meetings. Another dean had to vigorously advocate for more resources, including the help of an outside consultant, to deal with the continuous erosion of funds for administrative staff, which had caused serious schoolwide morale problems. In each case, it took us time to realize that we had to continuously solicit the support of the person to whom we reported because others on campus were competing for the same scarce resources of funding and central administration support.

Another regular theme involved building and maintaining an administrative staff. Fostering teamwork among career university employees, especially clerical staff, was a major challenge. In some cases, relationships were so strained that services to students and faculty were seriously affected. In other cases, there had been no previous support and recognition of excellent job performance. In each school many hours were spent addressing such teamwork issues as installing new computer systems, planning school events, coordinating with university administrators, remodeling the school building, and handling student concerns.

After the first few years, as we settled into our administrative routines, we could devote more time to alumni and student relations. In some cases, there had been very little written communication with alumni. In other cases, there was open hostility that needed to be addressed. In some schools, alumni were suspicious of the new dean and had to be reassured that the school's traditions would continue to be honored. In other schools, there was a strong desire to make sure that faculty exposed students to the changing realities of practice. In each school, support systems had to be built to provide staff support for alumni relations, update rosters and publications, launch fundraising activities, and plan annual alumni conferences.

Student relations also needed attention. When there was substantial student unrest and student task force reports, some of us were the targets of strongly felt protests. If there was no forum for student concerns, faculty-student committees and town hall meetings were developed. For curriculum, we found it necessary to frame student concerns in a format that would facilitate communications. Student complaints about individual instructors and courses also needed to be handled with care, balancing legitimate student perceptions with faculty prerogatives. In many cases, our biggest challenge was to establish communication mechanisms to help students direct their desires for constructive organizational change and improvement into committees that could address them. Frequently, students graduated before they could see or experience the fruits of their labors. Because students spend such limited time on campus and frequently must juggle the demands of school, work, and family, deans have little opportunity to get to know students. The only students who receive our full attention are those in trouble and those who seek us out. In our support group discussions, we regularly explored ways to foster the improvement of both student and alumni relations.

Endings and New Beginnings

As we approached our seventh year as deans, we discovered that it was a time of endings and new beginnings. As we began to plan again for the future, more questions arose. Following are some examples.

- What is the best way to build on successes and plan for the school's future?
- How do we stabilize the school climate affected by faculty promotions and new arrivals and departures?
- How do we solidify a structure of ongoing research funding and long-term fundraising?

- How do we move from a preoccupation with internal issues to a more proactive approach to external public issues?
- Where are each of us headed with respect to the next stages in our careers?
- How do we handle recurring problems?

As we each completed five years of service, the support-group discussions began to shift from dealing with the present to dealing with the future. In one school, central administration requested a new five-year plan. We had all begun a personal process of reviewing what we had accomplished, where we fell short of our goals, and our unfinished business. Our shared successes included increased enrollments, new faculty recruited, new programs established, and budgets either stabilized or growing. We realized that our own efforts to recognize each other's accomplishments were extremely important in a university environment where little appreciation is expressed, publicly or privately. Such mutual recognition and support empowered us to speculate about the future and project new horizons.

For one member, the next horizon involved a fifth-year review as part of a seven-year appointment that could be renewed for five additional years. This review coincided with an offer of a full professorship at a university in his hometown, which he accepted contingent on completing his seven-year term as dean. For others, it was a time of consolidating gains and organizational restructuring. In one case, one member of the group asked another to serve as an organizational consultant to assess the school's structure and make recommendations. In another instance, a dean was asked by his university to incorporate a substantial university research center into the school's structure. Much of the restructuring placed new demands and pressures on each of the deans.

Each of us had acquired considerable stature on our campuses and in one case had become the senior dean on campus in terms of length of service. For those of us who continued in the deanship role, new initiatives were under way that included collaborative projects in the community and overseas as well as new research project funding where the seeds had been planted years in advance. In addition to these transitions, stabilization was a major theme in the support-group discussions. After several years of faculty recruitment and promotions, it was time to stabilize the personnel system. This was particularly challenging in situations where junior faculty did not get promoted, usually with justifiable cause, and senior faculty experienced anxiety over their promotion applications. We each were confronted with difficult situations when faculty records of achievement fell short of campuswide standards. We each sought to advocate for our faculty and expended accumulated credits and goodwill to assist with the promotion process.

At the same time, we each sought to solidify a new infrastructure to support faculty research through a combination of school funds, foundation and research grants, and contracts with local agencies. The many hours of prospecting for resources over the previous five to six years began to pay off as faculty research grants were funded and alumni donations and endowment activity increased. Each of us had been cultivating relationships with potential donors over the years and were able to share our frustrations about how much energy and time is required to foster these relationships with such uncertain outcomes. We all realized that the rewards for such prospecting would be reaped by our successors.

The biggest challenge during this phase of endings and new beginnings was to make the transition from a predominantly internal focus on administrative issues and reaccreditation to a more external focus on the local, national, and international issues facing the profession. We had come full circle from our initial discussions about the future of the profession seven years earlier. Making speeches, meeting with local politicians and other government officials, and serving on high-profile community commissions and university committees were seen as important new initiatives designed to increase the school's visibility on campus and in the community. Our external environments also had changed. In 1985 we were affected by the Reagan cuts and anti-welfare sentiments. By 1992 we had a new Democrat in the White House and a new commitment to serve people in need.

The many challenges inherent in balancing internal and external relations provided much fodder for discussion. Using the deanship as a bully pulpit to speak out on important issues had been common among deans of an earlier generation when enrollments and budgets were growing and faculty were less contentious. However, engaging in public discourse required extra hours of weekend and evening duty. We all gave this activity high priority but we also found it difficult to derive much satisfaction from the increased sense of responsibility. For one of us, frustration hit an all-time high when he was criticized by his faculty for spending too much time on these outside activities.

The joy of sharing and telling about our personal challenges was enhanced throughout the seven years by attending national meetings two days early so our support group could meet. These special times supplemented the quarterly day-long meetings on each other's campuses. Therefore, it was with increasing sadness that we recognized that our support group was coming to an end with the departure of one member. Each of us was sustained, in part, by the realization that something special had been shared over the years that we would never forget and that this volume would serve as a partial continuation of our unique peer support experience.

Assessing the Impact of Peer Support

The support group provided an outlet for us to share frustrations in a confidential environment and it created a setting in which we could learn from one another. The learning was enriched by the fact that each of us was confronting different experiences that were unique to our own school as well as sharing experiences that were similar in all schools. This helped us realize that we were not alone in handling daily challenges. The most powerful aspect of the peer support group was that each member could find a safe harbor where he could step outside the culture of the dean and pursue a greater understanding of the internal and external forces at play. The support group also provided us an arena in which we could tell one another our deepest concerns and get emotional support. The group provided a forum to ask such questions as, How am I doing? and, How do I ask for and use outside consultation? It was a unique experience for men to be sharing openly and seeking guidance from other men.

The support group gave each member opportunities to step outside the culture of the dean. Each of us had spent fifteen or more years as a faculty member, so the transition to the deanship role was exciting and perplexing. The excitement derived from the opportunity to address key social work education and research issues while helping to shape the direction of an institution. The perplexing parts of the job were the daily assaults on the office of the dean by faculty, alumni, students, and community agency representatives. For example, it is not easy for agency staff and directors to understand that the dean is not a free agent when it comes to the faculty domain of curriculum change or the university's requirements for overhead charges to cover the cost of doing business with organizations off campus. Similarly, students and alumni expect that complaints deposited in the dean's office should receive immediate, unilateral responses, ignoring the fact that faculty or administrative staff have to be consulted. The most perplexing dilemmas are posed by faculty who lobby the dean for special favors or make demands that the dean deal with the troubling behaviors of other colleagues.

One of the first insights to be gleaned from the support group was the important distinction between person and role. When faculty or students or alumni enter the dean's office to share a concern, they want to talk to the dean, not necessarily the person in the role of the dean. This realization made each of us more comfortable sharing ideas knowing that the perception of the role of dean was more important than the persona of the incumbent. Then we realized that people who had a grievance simply wanted a hearing from the dean, not necessarily an immediate response or to be involved in solving the problem. By selectively using the problem-solving process and emphasizing empathetic listening, it became much easier to balance the person and the role. It took several support group sessions to acquire this insight into academic administration.

Many times the support-group agenda included discussions about the culture of faculty behavior. This view from the dean's office differed substantially from the collegial view acquired over our years as faculty members. Tensions emerged between dean and faculty in hiring priorities, group responsibility for reaccreditation self-study, and fostering a climate of teamwork and sharing. In one case, the dean confronted the faculty as a group to clarify curriculum content and the school's future directions. Another dean found some faculty members' behavior counterproductive to fostering a climate of collegiality and fairness to students, so he developed an organizational credo statement, spelling out the purpose and values of the school. The credo was discussed at a faculty retreat, and deemed unnecessary and not worthy of adoption by the faculty.

The most striking aspects of the support group were its intensity and trust. Although an entire day was devoted to an evolving agenda, it was clear by the end of the day that there wasn't time to address everything on the agenda. However, at the end of each session we all felt that our batteries had been recharged by sharing difficult situations and acquiring new perspectives on immediate concerns. No one wanted to miss the next meeting.

The informal sharing between meetings was also significant—sharing information about national issues, faculty hiring prospects, university policies and procedures, funding opportunities. Two of us developed a joint public agency training program, and shared guest lecturers and community events.

We all were surprised, in hindsight, at our collective tacit understandings about the confidential nature of sharing, the array of issues held in common, the absence of conflict or significant disagreement, and the great trust achieved early in the support group's development. The support group meetings provided a forum for self-discovery about our progress toward our shared goal of being successful and helping our schools become outstanding institutions. It obviously helped that we were only a three-person group, our schools were so close, we are the same sex, and nearly the same age, and we came to the group as equals having started our tenure as deans at the same time.

We also spent considerable time discussing career aspirations as new job opportunities arose for one or more of us. We each worried about overstaying our welcomes, especially in the light of deans who stayed in office more than twelve years (in one of our institutions, there was a policy of twelve years maximum for deans). Our candid discussions always raised questions about the tenure of a dean, how much organizational change is possible, and doubts about how much of one's efforts could ever be fully understood and appreciated by others. These discussions produced immense catharsis and reaffirmation of each other.

As we approached our seventh year as deans, we began to realize that the group would change when one of us moved out of the area to return to teaching and research (Austin and Gilmore, 1993). To help us deal with the termination of the groups we decided to try to capture, in written case studies, our experiences guiding organizational change. For our departing member, the case study represented an ending; for our other two the case study afforded an opportunity to take stock and identify new beginnings. The process of writing and sharing drafts was simply one more attempt by the members to step outside the culture of the deanship to chronicle the experiences as objectively as possible as well as to relate some of the lessons we had learned. This process challenged us as practicing administrators to find the time and the conceptual framework within which to capture the excitement and dilemmas of organizational leadership. The peer support group also provided one member with the ideas and concepts to address the entry and exit phases of administrative life (Austin, 1989).

References

Austin, M. J. "Executive Entry: Multiple Perspectives on the Process of Muddling Through." *Administration in Social Work,* 1989, *13* (4), 55–71.

Austin, M. J., and Gilmore, T. N. "Executive Exit: Multiple Perspectives on Managing the Leadership Transition." *Administration in Social Work,* 1993, *17* (1), 47–60.

MICHAEL J. AUSTIN *is professor in the School of Social Welfare at the University of California, Berkeley and dean emeritus of the School of Social Work at the University of Pennsylvania.*

To publish or perish has as much to do with a faculty member's
research and teaching abilities as it does with a professional school
dean's ability to advocate for the unique knowledge-building activities
of a profession.

The Role of the Dean in Strengthening Faculty and Student Scholarship

Rino J. Patti

As I read the experiences recounted in these pages I find myself nodding in agreement, sympathizing with my colleagues, sharing their anger, excitement, and exhaustion, and sometimes reliving episodes that occurred during my deanship.

The notion that deanships evolve through distinctive phases accords with my experience. For me, however, the beginning was longer and the end, which is beginning to take shape, will not come for another year, when I plan to step down. The idea that the culture of a faculty and school does much to shape the dean's options is certainly fundamental to my experience as well. It is also true that the dean is in some sense marginal to most of the groups with which he or she works—a part of, but also apart from, virtually everyone. That is probably necessary, because much of the job involves mediating between, and sometimes aligning, different constituencies to pursue common goals. A sense of marginality, and its close relative loneliness, was also a part of my experience. The account in Chapter Four almost made me feel as if I had been a member of the three-dean support group, yet sad that I had not been. One idea the deans imply, but don't develop in depth, is that of the dean as strategist. I would like to explore this facet of the decanal landscape, using my experience of building the scholarly portfolio of one school. My concern here is the evolution of a long, linked strategy. Over eight years I sought to augment the quantity and quality of the faculty's scholarship and ultimately change the assumptions and values regarding the school's scholarly mission.

I started with a strategy for how to encourage scholarly work based largely on my experience as a faculty member, and that strategy changed over time as

NEW DIRECTIONS FOR HIGHER EDUCATION, no. 98, Summer 1997 © Jossey-Bass Publishers

tactics failed or succeeded, faculty came and went, competing priorities emerged, and political and fiscal constraints and opportunities rose and receded. My direction led to several crises that required rethinking my tactics. In retrospect, the shaping of the strategy was more akin to a prolonged Easter egg hunt in an unmarked patch than a game of chess played by a master. What stayed constant throughout was a keen desire to expand the scholarly work of the faculty and raise the national standing of the school.

Shaping a Strategy: The First Five Years

In the interviews leading to my appointment and shortly after my arrival the faculty was, as might be expected, keenly interested in my vision for the school. I believed and said on many occasions that building faculty scholarship was a principal goal. In early meetings and reports, I told the provost that the school could be in the top five nationally if we built the research and publication profile of the faculty. This was to be the centerpiece of my administration. Reorganizing the doctoral program, raising money for the research center, modifying the faculty's heavy committee and teaching loads to allow time for more research, identifying collaborative research opportunities, and supporting the junior faculty were key elements in my plan.

In the early years of my tenure as dean I worked on several fronts to strengthen the school's research and scholarly capability. The following policy initiatives were intended to shift incentives and reward structures to encourage faculty involvement in scholarly activities.

- Reduce faculty work loads, from five to four courses a year to free time for scholarly activities, without any specific expectations for increased publication or grant activity.
- Allow faculty members to buy out of up to half their course load with funded research.
- Revise tenure and promotion guidelines to clarify and strengthen the scholarly requirements for promotion to associate professor.
- Assess and strengthen the doctoral program to improve student research preparation, develop specializations earlier, link course work more closely with the dissertation, and increase funding to support doctoral students.
- Establish a program of collaborative research with community agencies, using small grants to faculty that would be matched by the agencies to support pilot projects that could be used as a basis for submitting proposals to foundations and federal agencies.
- Revise the faculty workload formula to give workload credit for teaching doctoral tutorials.

The objective results of these policy initiatives were significant, but not dramatic. The number of publications produced by the faculty each year increased incrementally, but the relative national standing of the school on this measure did not improve. Likewise, the number of citations to faculty publications as reflected in the social science citation index also increased, but here, too, the results were modest.

Several major research projects were funded during these years and the number of smaller research grants grew steadily. Indeed, between 1989 and 1994, research grants to the faculty increased from less than \$1 million to more than \$3 million. Altogether the faculty was more actively engaged in research, and other kinds of scholarship such as textbooks, policy- and issue-oriented books, and theoretically oriented work also increased.

Perhaps most impressive were changes in the doctoral program. The curriculum was modified to strengthen research preparation and allow students to pursue more individualized courses of study through tutorials with faculty members. Closely associated with individualized courses of study and the opportunity to specialize was the growing practice of employing doctoral students as research assistants on faculty projects. Whether cause or effect, more students began to matriculate full-time with the goal of preparing for academic careers.

But amid the progress were disappointments. Despite clear expectations regarding the necessity for publications, several assistant professors did not progress satisfactorily, their mid-term reviews indicating that they were unlikely to achieve tenure at the end of their probation. Though excellent instructors, senior faculty members agreed that the candidates' scholarly productivity was inadequate. These experiences, stretching over several years, provoked the faculty to reexamine hiring criteria and moved the faculty to pay at least as much attention to candidates' scholarly preparation and capacity as to their teaching ability.

Faculty Process: Contest and Division

Efforts to strengthen the scholarship also sharpened political and ideological divisions within the school. The faculty had not been known for open factionalism and its members prided themselves on being friendly and supportive to colleagues, working through disagreements and seeking compromises whenever contentious issues threatened division and alienation. They deferred to minority opinion and slowed the decision processes whenever there was active opposition to a new policy or direction. My predilection to mediate and compromise was consistent with this normative system. At the same time, I and others felt it important to press on with efforts to increase the scholarly productivity of the school.

These two forces—the desire to maintain the interpersonal norms and the desire to move the school forward—competed with one another over these five years. My role increasingly became one of trying to strike a balance between the forces that would allow the school to move forward, while maintaining the spirit of collegiality the faculty and I valued.

Throughout the first four to five years, a number of issues generated sharp disagreement and served as focal points for the faculty to develop coalitions or factions. One of the most important issues was the definition of scholarship. I define scholarship broadly, but several faculty members felt that empirical research was the implicit standard for scholarship. Those whose work was more theoretical and conceptual and based on bibliographic research argued that their scholarship was valued less highly. On the face of it, those with funded research did appear to be advantaged because they often had funds to buy out of teaching, hire doctoral assistants, and purchase equipment, whereas other faculty members could not. Moreover, their work tended to be more readily recognized within the university community and, some felt, within the school. The few faculty members whose research was funded came to be seen as privileged, a perception fed by a sense that the research center resources were being allocated disproportionately to assist faculty members who pursued funded research.

Although some faculty members felt that they were being pressured to write proposals that would bring funds to the school, and others were concerned about the impact of course buyouts for research on the teaching workloads of other faculty, perhaps the most troublesome problem during these early years was a faculty perception that the doctoral program director, the research center director, and the dean were somehow engaged in a coordinated effort to preempt faculty decision-making prerogatives. Some feared that these two faculty members were exercising undue influence on a variety of decisions and that this exercise of power was sanctioned, and even encouraged, by the dean.

In a faculty that values harmony and civility, this tension was widely seen as a problem. In spring 1993, a consultant was retained to guide a retreat at which these issues could be addressed. A great many concerns and problems were aired, many of which had only a tangential relationship to the issues discussed here. Specifics aside, the retreat seemed mostly concerned with trust, equity, and process. Trust concerned the need to know or feel that important issues were being aired openly and that decisions were not being "steered." Equity had to do with seeing that resources were allocated fairly, using criteria that all understood. Out of the retreat also emerged a reaffirmation of the importance of a governance process guided by norms and procedures shared by the faculty.

As for me, I learned that if the dean is to have the confidence of the faculty, he or she must be seen as a dean of all the faculty. No matter the intent, the perception that certain faculty members are in league with the dean erodes this confidence. At some point, if the social integration of the faculty matters, the advocacy of a policy or direction may have to be moderated until deep differences can be mediated. The next two years was a time to digest and integrate the changes occurring in the culture of the school.

Modifying the Strategy: The Second Term

As I began my second term, I felt keenly the limitations of a dean to change the culture of a faculty. I became increasingly convinced that achieving lasting change regarding the value of scholarship in the life of the school would be a slower process than I ever imagined. In particular, at this juncture, it seemed that such a change would require more than simply supporting faculty members one by one in their respective pursuits and more than creating an infrastructure to support research. Increasingly, I thought that the key element was emergence of a belief system that made scholarly inquiry in all its forms a central mission of the faculty, a powerful expectation that colleagues had of one another. This would mean working more closely with the faculty, especially those who for various reasons did not consider this priority important.

The beginning of my second five-year term coincided with the appointment of a new provost. A physicist from a prestigious private eastern university, the new provost immediately signaled that he would be much more interested than his predecessor in the academic quality of the university's schools and colleges. From the outset he made it clear that only those schools demonstrating excellence could expect to survive. With a mandate from the president to raise the university into the very top ranks of private universities, he began immediately to develop a strategic plan that would build on and extend the unique characteristics of the institution.

During this period, 1993 to 1995, there were several developments that bode well for the scholarly mission of the school. The national ranking of schools of social work published by *U.S. News & World Report* in March 1994 placed the school seventh among all graduate programs in the country. Several new junior faculty were recruited from top doctoral programs, all of whom appeared to have considerable potential as research scholars. Enrollment in the master's program continued to increase, as did tuition revenues. Indirect cost recovery on research and training grants also grew rapidly. The additional income permitted several enhancements with research-supporting potential: computers were upgraded and hard wired to the university system and the Internet; a computer technician was hired to provide technical assistance to the faculty; a fund of $750 a year was established for each faculty member to be used to support his or her scholarship; consultations and trainings were arranged to update the faculty on advanced statistical techniques; increased support in doing literature searches for grant proposals was provided to the faculty. These and other enhancements were generally well received by the faculty, though as always needs remained a step ahead of the outcome of these investments.

By the fall of 1995, findings from several recent studies of journal publications indicated that the faculty ranked somewhere between tenth and eighteenth among all schools, depending on the methodology employed. Analyses of the publication record for this period showed a small increase in the articles in peer-reviewed journals, but the per capita publication rate had remained largely constant. Encouraging was the increased number of books produced by senior faculty. In addition, although good data were not available, it appeared that the school was probably not keeping pace with other top ten schools in the amount of sponsored research. There were, in fact, a significant number of research projects being conducted by faculty, but most were small investigations and many were internally funded. In part, this was due to the fact that a third of the faculty members (eight of twenty-five) were assistant professors whose work was in the pilot stage.

In the fall of 1995, I decided to bring to the faculty a plan for moving the school into the very top ranks of schools of social work. To the extent that the school was perceived as national leader in its field, it would benefit from increased university development and public relations support, thus further strengthening its position within the university. In my mind, augmenting the scholarship of the faculty had always been a key to improving the national standing of the school. After much faculty discussion and debate, a multifaceted plan emerged that involved a number of initiatives calculated to advance the school's national standing.

- Hiring a senior person with a record of federally funded mental health research.
- Conducting annual goal-setting meetings with faculty to set scholarly goals and individualized plans for achieving them.
- Hiring a person to administer the research center and provide technical assistance.
- Setting a collective annual goal for faculty publication in peer-reviewed journals and books.
- Setting a goal of three federally funded research projects in the school with a projected rate of indirect cost recovery.
- Setting a goal of full funding of doctoral students.

Though unanimously adopted by the faculty, it is difficult to know how successfully the plan will be implemented. Perhaps most important, the faculty seems be evolving a new collective sense of the importance of scholarship to the life and future of the school.

Conclusion

It is hazardous to generalize from a single case. Each school has its own history and culture, and interpersonal chemistry. External environments vary in significant ways. This case and others reported in this volume demonstrate the difficulty of changing organizational cultures in academic settings. Certainly, deans can play a role in this transformation, but typically power, resources, and discretion are too broadly shared in the academy to permit one person to bring about such fundamental changes. Rather it seems that the dean's role is to suggest new ideas, challenge existing assumptions and patterns of behavior, and seek to engineer consensus around new or at least differently prioritized values and norms. In the best of circumstances, the dean has the active support of a few influential faculty leaders, a supportive university administration, and a beneficent market. In the end, however, culture change occurs when a significant number of faculty members begin to believe that both individual and collective interests are better served by doing business in different ways. Exactly how that occurs is still somewhat of a mystery, but several elements are suggested by the case presented here.

Perhaps most critical is the salient scholarship goal itself. The critical importance of good scholarship to inform practice and policy development is a widely held value, though not always a top priority in schools of social work. The strategic importance of augmented scholarship for the future position of the school in the university was, or became, apparent to most of the faculty.

The case reported here suggests that an old, well-entrenched culture may need to be unfrozen before the process of change can begin. At the outset I assumed that the existing culture would support efforts to build scholarship and that only capacity-building and support were necessary to bring this about. After several years it became clear that more was at issue than simply resources. An earlier attempt at unfreezing, perhaps a strategic-planning process, might have been useful as a way of assessing how receptive the faculty culture was to the idea of making scholarship more central to the school's mission.

An important catalyst in cultural change appears to be the dean's persistence in advocating a goal. Schools must do many things to succeed and it is tempting, indeed sometimes convenient, to shift priorities. In a loosely coupled system it is often difficult to get the faculty's attention, let alone mobilize them around an organizational goal. Staying with a goal, in this case augmenting the scholarship of the faculty, allows for continuity in the change process.

Although goal constancy is important, so too is strategic adaptability. As this case demonstrated, it was necessary at several points to rethink and modify the strategy. There is a temptation to become enamored of a particular approach to change and to proceed with it in the face of significant resistance. Listening to the reasons underlying the resistance and refashioning strategy to address these issues seems preferable to moving into the storm at full throttle.

When important professional interests such as the value placed on various types of scholarship are involved, faculty governance processes can become highly politicized. At times like these, it becomes important to avoid partisan alliances with certain groups of faculty, because to do so means losing the ability to act as a mediator and resolver of conflict. Although aligning with a faculty faction may result in a political victory, the loss of trust and resulting damage to the social fabric of the faculty can have more serious long-term ramifications for cultural cohesion. If the group becomes sharply factionalized, the task of building a new, widely shared culture becomes infinitely more difficult.

RINO J. PATTI is dean of the School of Social Work at the University of Southern California, Los Angeles.

Is the dean the master or servant of the faculty? Whatever the answer,
it pays for deans not to take themselves too seriously.

Getting Chalk: Distant Reflections on Deaning

Stuart A. Kirk

One reason that a dean's authority is difficult to acquire is because it is earned only by meeting the expectations of diverse constituencies, and the expectations of university administration, faculty, students, and community representatives are not just different, they often are inconsistent. The administration wants an experienced manager and strong leader who will bring further prominence to the university, impress and woo the corporate and foundation worlds and bring in millions of dollars, run a tidy academic shop, and keep the inevitable messy internal problems of the school from seeping out into the broader university or community arena where the odor becomes a distraction or problem for the central administration.

The faculty, which rarely speaks with one mind, wants a dean who will make the university administration's life harder, not easier. All faculties tend to feel that their school is not getting a fair share of the university's resources and that the administration is more interested in bureaucratic tidiness and upbeat press releases than academic freedom and intellectual creativity. The faculty wants a dean to defend scholars, to appreciate and respect scholarship and teaching, and to represent vigorously his or her school's special interests in competition with the other schools on campus and against the imposing power of the central administration. The dean's job, as one colleague aptly put it, is to keep chalk in the classrooms.

The professional community is itself diverse and often has surprisingly little understanding of how differently universities are governed than governmental or corporate organizations. For example, the professionals usually fail to appreciate the limited authority and prerogatives of deans. Yet, they have their own priority tasks for the new dean. Usually, they expect the dean to bridge the gap between the isolated and introspective proclivities of academia and the chaotic, worldly, and expertise-hungry world on the other side of the metaphorical moat.

Students have the least understanding of what a dean does, but, like other constituencies, are not shy about sharing their preferences. A dean should be available to students, shape the curriculum and course schedule to their needs, increase financial aid, get rid of poor instructors and grant tenure to their favorite teachers, upgrade the student lounge, and ensure that they all get good-paying jobs when they graduate. The dean is also expected to be readily available for coffee and casual conversation.

It is little wonder, when one becomes a dean, that a support group is useful, as it was to the authors of Chapter Four of this volume, who shared their decanal stories with each other over seven years and now with us. These stories brought back vividly my own saga and the complicated, chaotic, and fast-paced process of deaning. One encounters relatively few such autobiographical accounts in the literature, so these tales stimulated my distant and undisturbed memories about the challenges and triumphs of deaning.

Their stories provide many examples of most deans' common experiences: initial enthusiasm and dedication; the uses of organizational and political skill and creativity; the difficulties of managing one's time; the need for perseverance and stamina; the inevitability of personal pain and disappointment, as well as of naivete. Anyone who is considering becoming a dean can learn a great deal from these stories about trying to guide change in academic organizations. At the same time, many topics are only partially explored, but nonetheless are important to the experience of deaning. I want to comment about several. The following observations are based largely on my personal experience, admittedly a shaky foundation for generalization.

Why Become a Dean?

In the Editors' Notes at the beginning of this volume, the question, Why would anyone accept a deanship? is asked. The question is not answered satisfactorily. The authors of the various chapters offer the conventional wisdom: for career advancement, higher salary, more prestige, perks, to create change. In telling their own stories the authors say very little about what drove them to apply for or accept their deanships. Whatever the merits of the conventional explanations about motivations to be a dean, they rarely constitute a full answer. In fact, they provide hardly any answer at all. For example, virtually every faculty member wants advancement, money, prestige, and perks. And virtually all want some aspects of their organizations to change. Nevertheless, few want to be a dean! Why not? And why do those few seek such a position? Is it that their desire for advancement, money, or prestige is greater? I doubt it.

The immediate joys of a deanship do not offer a convincing explanation either. In fact, the descriptions of these deans' jobs are pretty gruesome. One author vividly describes what he inherited: low and declining enrollments, ineffective student recruitment, a long-standing leadership vacuum, neglected and decaying facilities, shabby offices, antiquated office equipment, unfilled positions, budget deficits, a looming mandatory accreditation review, a need for curriculum revisions, deteriorated relations with alumni and the community, relatively low level of faculty scholarship, and questionable support, if not hostility, from the university administration. Hardly the material for a deanship advertisement in the *Chronicle of Higher Education* that would elicit a stampede for the job or generate enthusiasm, dedication, or inspiration from a new appointee. Thus, the question: Why seek such a job when there are so many good reasons (apparent to most faculty members) to avoid it?

There is no one answer to this question. People become deans like people become ship captains or cops—for many different reasons, some intensely personal. Certainly, many people desire to be dean to be a leader in their field. But there are other motivations. I know of individuals who sought, or at least accepted, a deanship out of a deep sense of personal loyalty to a particular institution; out of a need to return to a region in the country where they had family ties; out of anger and frustration with their current institution and their desire to reject it by going elsewhere; out of a need to get away from a troublesome marriage or relationship; out of a deep sense of uncertainty about their personal competence and their need to prove publicly their abilities; out of a desire to escape from the classroom, where their performance was undistinguished and personally unsatisfying; out of a need to prove that they could be much better at deaning than the deans they previously served under and fought with; out of a need to avoid the constant burden of being a productive scholar; and out of the sensible desire to move to a better climate.

These less conventional motivations affect to some extent the ability of new deans to carry on in the face of adversity, to find the inner strength to follow through and succeed. A little money, a title, and a parking space carry a new dean only so far—but not far enough to carry through years of marathon administrative meetings, budgets that never quite cover required expenditures, clerical staff intransigence, needless bickering among faculty, and the awareness that you can never do enough. And deans cannot gain sustenance from colleagues, because rarely does anyone tell them they are doing a good job. So their initial motivations to become a dean must be strong and personally convincing.

Scholarship and Organizational Culture

The problem of scholarship and organizational culture comes up repeatedly in the authors' discussions. They describe their attempts to increase faculty productivity, their anguish over making tough promotion and tenure decisions and hiring new faculty, the university pressure to have a research-active faculty, and the dissension among faculty about the relative importance of publication versus other indicators of performance.

There is little doubt that major universities expect schools to produce research and reward faculty that do. Universities depend on the grant and contract money that research-active faculty attract and they enjoy the prestige that accumulates from a faculty that fills the pages of the nation's major scientific and intellectual journals. Furthermore, part of the core mission of major research universities is to "advance knowledge," an effort that all faculty members are expected to participate in. The expectation is codified in the criteria for promotion and tenure. Universities expect deans to champion these standards, and they usually do.

On the other hand, and readily apparent in the authors' descriptions of the culture of their schools of social work (as in some schools that I am familiar with), their faculties often would prefer that a dean protect them from these standards, which they feel are alien, inappropriate, and unjust. They want the dean to justify to the university why social work is different and should be exempt, to buffer the faculty from the university's harsh application of scientific criteria in personnel decisions. The deans in these situations are uncomfortably caught between two cultures, neither of which is likely to change much during the dean's tenure.

Nevertheless, these authors all tried to reorient their faculty into a research direction. And, if progress can be made in this realm, it cannot be made without the dean's active, consistent, and firm leadership. A dean is uniquely able to encourage scholarship—not just in word, but in deed—by restructuring workloads, allocating research assistance, demonstrating respect and appreciation for the achievements of productive faculty members, hiring research-oriented faculty members, and by being tough-minded in upholding the university's standards for promotion and tenure. Though each such effort is a very small step, each move can be expected to elicit opposition from some faculty members. The new dean is typically accused of pandering to the administration, devaluing teaching and community service, or of threatening the traditional values of the school, if not of social work in general. These are not easy accusations to handle. But an effective dean has little choice. The school's long-term health and survival depends on its reputation within the university as an academically sound and productive member of the community of scholars. A dean who neglects this task does not serve the school well.

The Best Laid Plans

I was reminded by these case histories of making plans and implementing them, of how often deans, like other mortals, must adjust to unexpected events. A supportive (or feared) vice president or president departs or arrives; key members of the faculty retire, resign, become gravely ill or die; enrollments rise or fall sharply; students accuse the school administration of gender or racial discrimination or insensitivity; a donor suddenly appears wanting to make a major gift; the state tax revenues fall short and the governor takes an ax to the university's budget; a few disgruntled faculty members seek a vote of confidence in the leadership; a student accuses a faculty member of sexual harassment and threatens to sue; or your own health or that of a close family member requires immediate and sustained attention.

Every dean can expect to confront these unexpected developments. In fact, every dean who lasts more than a few years will experience most of these events and more. The problem is that deans won't know when, who, what, or how much until they are confronted with the event that will demand they put aside their carefully developed plan, at least temporarily, and reassess what needs to be done now. Serendipity and fate are the dean's unappointed comrades, sometimes helping move the school along its intended trajectory, at other times diverting it. Discussions of planning and guiding organizational change have at their core the assumption that deliberate executive action can make a noticeable difference, and I certainly concur. But we also need a full discussion of the unexpected and its challenges to effective leadership.

Role Modeling

Deans often have the decidedly awkward task of touting the centrality and sanctity of teaching and research while doing none of it themselves. Of course, deans sometimes have exemplary teaching and research records from their faculty days, but few continue to contribute as teachers and scholars in the face of the assault on their time from the demands of being deans. The authors of these case studies, scholars of some note prior to becoming deans, say almost nothing about their teaching and research activity while dean. Perhaps they understandably engaged in little while they undertook their enormous administrative tasks. Or perhaps they continued, but have just not mentioned it in this volume, viewing it as irrelevant to their work as deans. This would be a mistake, I think, for several reasons.

Many able faculty members successfully avoid major administrative appointments, because they cherish their time to read and write and assume that being dean will end their careers as active scholars. When deans don't continue to engage in some scholarly work, they confirm these suspicions of the very members of the faculty from whom thoughtful leadership might emerge in the future.

But the costs of abandoning the life of a scholar are more personal, as well. Deaning can be a lonely, demanding, and frustrating endeavor. For example, months or years of curriculum planning, discussions, and persuasion can end up marooned on faculty prerogatives or sunk by a stingy campus budget committee. The dean, who is ostensibly in control, often has little control beyond what thoughtfulness and persistence might extract from various constituencies. There are many moments in the lives of all deans when initiatives stall, when their frustration with the daily grind mounts, when their energy is sapped, when their political allies waver, and when they wonder whether their efforts are worth it.

I found that at those times I needed to retreat for a day or so to my research and writing. Call it therapy. It was a way to remind myself of my interrupted first calling, to gain sustenance by escaping into a world of ideas and issues far removed from university budgets, personnel decisions, or cranky faculty, to exert some control over some minor research project or manuscript, to gain a sense of making progress on something, and to assure myself that deaning was by no means my sole source of professional satisfaction. During most years, I taught a course for many of the same reasons. I never wanted to feel trapped in a deanship, as some become, able to acquire loads of chalk and have it delivered to classrooms, but never able to use it again.

Personal salvation is not the only benefit of staying alive as a scholar. In the eyes of both the senior and untenured faculty, a dean who is contributing to scholarship enjoys increased legitimacy and influence. This is especially the case if the dean's goals include increasing the faculty's research productivity. Deans who make the time to continue to write and teach, as some do, demonstrate their dedication to these core functions of the university. Their high expectations for faculty performance have added weight, because they are espousing principles that they themselves abide by. This role modeling can be an important aspect of academic leadership, although it is rarely highlighted.

The Difference a Dean Makes

The schools of social work that these authors discuss, like most academic units, survive and change whether the leadership is good or not. If effective leadership at the school or department level were a requirement for organizational survival, universities would be barren places, full of empty, stately buildings serving as silent monuments to former lousy administrators. To a new dean this may be a depressing thought, suggesting that individual efforts may have limited impact. Or it might be a reassuring observation, since it also suggests that a dean cannot do too much harm; that no matter what mistakes are made, the school will somehow muddle through and survive.

In these case studies, there is an inevitable tendency to showcase achievements: curriculum changes, reaccreditation, increased enrollments, acquisition of new equipment, new productive faculty, and strengthened ties with alumni or the community. And there is the unspoken assumption that it was the deliberate action of the dean that made all of that happen. But some of those changes were bound to occur anyway. For example, student enrollments in social work dropped everywhere in the early 1980s, then magically sprang back nationally. Curricula are always in evolution as faculty change, new ideas and problems emerge, and faculty tinker with their course arrangements. Mandatory reviews for reaccreditation are usually tremendous threats to new deans and they take, as I certainly did, great pride in ushering a school through it successfully. But realistically, no established school has actually lost its reaccreditation. Likewise, fancy telephone systems, high-quality copy machines, powerful personal computers and networks were bound to make their way into schools of social work, no matter how tardy their arrival.

I make these observations, not to denigrate any of the achievements of these deans—for they appear to have accomplished much against the odds—but to suggest that a distinction could be made between changes that might have occurred anyway and those that, in all likelihood, would not have occurred without the special energy and commitment of a particular dean.

There is another way to assess the difference a dean makes. Do the innovations, the programs, the customs, and the direction of the school that a dean has created and nurtured remain intact years after the dean has resigned? This, it seems to me, is the ultimate test of leadership. I have witnessed deans who were, on the surface, remarkably effective in changing a school, but whose handiwork was immediately dismantled after they departed. In contrast, I have also seen schools whose former leaders transformed those schools to such an extent that even decades afterward the schools still bear the unmistakable fingerprints of strong and creative former deans. What the test of time reveals is whether organizational change was institutionalized, not just cosmetic, whether the culture of the place was permanently altered, and whether what took place under the guidance of a particular dean transcended that person's personality and temporary authority by becoming rooted in the views and habits of many faculty.

Conclusion

The deanly stories in this volume are useful and unmistakably real. But they might not, I have been stumbling to say, contain the whole truth. For example, I have a tendency when reminiscing about my years as dean to recollect them in heroic terms: the dedication and altruism that I took to the new job; the terrible state of affairs that I inherited; the creativity and stamina with which I met the enormous and complex obstacles that had to be overcome; the cascade of my wonderful accomplishments; and my uncommon wisdom in knowing just when to resign after the mission was accomplished.

I really enjoy my story. Perhaps it would be more believable, however, if I acknowledged my own selfish motives, my many mistakes, the distortions of my vision, and the lingering problems that I left behind. Of course, unlike the three able deans who have shared their stories with us, I deliberately planned to leave a few messy problems behind, so the next new dean could complain about the terrible state of affairs.

STUART A. KIRK is Ralph and Marjorie Crump chair in the Department of Social Welfare, School of Public Policy and Social Research, University of California, Los Angeles, and is former dean of the School of Social Welfare, Rockefeller College of Public Affairs and Policy, State University of New York at Albany.

How many deans could have predicted that someday they would be asked to assume the role? Whatever the answer, few could anticipate the complexity of deaning in a large, highly rated, public research university.

Serving as Dean: A Public University Perspective

Paula Allen-Meares

The thoughtful chapters in this volume shed light on the complicated dimensions and aspects of the role of the dean in schools of social work. I have experienced many of the issues raised by my esteemed colleagues: struggling to be comprehensive and inclusive; being sandwiched between a variety of forces and groups; being viewed as a manager when my preference is to be a productive scholar and faculty member; hearing the many voices of the academic unit; tuning in to both implicit and explicit communications from a variety of sources; and being able to make tough decisions that rise above self-interest groups and politics.

I, too, backed into the role of dean; however, I am different from the other contributors to this volume. I am an African American female. Though one of the contributors is an African American male, I want to go on record that women in such leadership positions have unique experiences and struggles. Throughout the bureaucratic layers, men still dominate in administrative posts in higher education. Assumptions about women—their ability to lead, to make tough decisions, and to break through the male-dominated informal and formal networks to gain influence—still operate in the minds of some. It is even sadder to discover that some women colleagues, viewing themselves as liberated advocates of change, still question whether another woman can handle the job. Although support staff—still predominantly females—will enthusiastically support their male supervisors, my interaction with other female deans as well as personal experience leads me to believe that the same level of enthusiasm is not always available for women in comparable positions. I can recall one secretary commenting to another, "She should be home with her daughter; family

NEW DIRECTIONS FOR HIGHER EDUCATION, no. 98, Summer 1997 © Jossey-Bass Publishers

should come first." The implicit message here is that if you are a female and a dean you are neglecting your family or do not embrace the role of motherhood. Are men failures at the role of fatherhood because they are deans? I doubt it!

Both of my deanships have been with large public research universities. It is only fitting, therefore, that I reflect on this unique contextual environment, its mission and sometimes conflicting political and social agendas, and what I learned over the years. One university was not only the flagship research institution of a large, complex state system, it also had a land-grant mission and a focus on the hard sciences. The other institution, viewed by some as being more private than public, was known for its interdisciplinary nature and highly ranked social science departments and professional schools.

To be perfectly honest, I did not have a specific career plan to become a dean when the opportunity emerged. It just happened. In my discussions with male counterparts over the years, it has become increasingly clear to me that many of them have a career plan. They have thought strategically about what prerequisite managerial experiences and administrative posts would prepare them well for a deanship and lead to other leadership positions in higher education. The lack of a career plan could be unique to me and not apply to other women deans.

Background

When directing the doctoral program—my first major administrative post—at the University of Illinois, Urbana-Champaign, Dean Daniel Saunders nominated me for the special Leadership Program for women and minorities in higher education administration. This initiative, sponsored by the Committee on Institutional Cooperation, provided course work on changes in higher education, budget and financing, and other relevant information. I was unaware at the time that within a year the Executive Committee would nominate me to serve as interim dean of the School of Social Work following the sudden death of Dean Saunders. With support of the vice president for academic affairs and the faculty, I assumed the position.

After a national search was launched, I was nominated for the position, applied, and was offered the post for a five-year term. Immediately preceding my appointment, the need to enhance my theoretical understanding of how to manage an organization and how to enhance my leadership skills led me to Harvard University. I was nominated and then applied for a special program to prepare higher education leaders and was accepted there. Some of the conceptual content presented in the course work at Harvard has played a critical role in how I think and go about the business of managing and leading a school of social work in a public research university as we approach a new millennium.

Having completed my M.S.W. and Ph.D. degrees, successfully achieved promotion and tenure, and been appointed doctoral program director, then dean of the School of Social Work at the University of Illinois, Urbana-Champaign, I was very comfortable and responded less than enthusiastically when the University of Michigan called. However, the persistence of the university's search committee led me to say that I would visit, but that I was totally content with my current situation. Impressed with the opportunity to link social work with the social sciences and other professional units, I began to view the interesting possibilities. Before I knew it, I was off to take on a major assignment—a larger school with the added challenge of raising funds to build a new facility.

Concerned about how to increase effectiveness and which factors contribute to excellence in role performance, I had the pleasure as a member of the National Association of Deans and Directors of Schools of Social Work editorial committee to help prepare *The Administration of Social Work Education Programs: The Roles of Deans and Directors* (Raymond, 1995). In the preparation of the book, the committee surveyed deans nationwide to examine demographics, issues, and trends.

The survey also explored the correlates of job efficacy of deans. In the absence of an objective measure of role efficacy, two sets of measures were identified as dependent variables: external indicators of role success, and self-reported role satisfaction. Three sets of independent variables were used to predict role effectiveness: personal characteristics such as experience, demographic descriptors, and priorities and goals of the dean; organizational context, including program type, size, and autonomy; and role functioning, as in time allocation and leadership style. Multiple regressions of these variables found that situation-specific factors predicted a dean's success and satisfaction more than did personal characteristics, including reputation, experience, or prestige (see Videka-Sherman, Allen-Meares, and Yegidis, 1995). I found this result most interesting. Important variables for determining the dean's role effectiveness were organizational context; how the school is positioned within a given campus (for example, a free-standing unit); title of the academic leader (dean, department chair, director, or other); and university support. I also immediately noted that many of these variables were beyond the control of the dean to influence and change in order to maximize effective leadership.

Edward and Baskin's (1995) chapter on deans as successful academic leaders suggests that the individual must give clear directions, be comfortable playing multiple roles, stress goal attainment, be a human-relations specialist, and be able to build consensus. The models and styles of the leaders are as diverse as these abilities.

The Changing Landscape of the Public Research University

The pressures on the public research university are not unique to it: continuing budget pressures; changing demographics of the potential student pool; an aging infrastructure for education and research; shifting priorities after the cold war; continuing uneasiness about the loss of the United States' competitive advantage in international markets; a growing federal deficit, which affects states' budgets and certain state research universities; increasing urban poverty; and the diminishing middle class (see Patel, 1995).

The public has become somewhat disenchanted with the dominance of the research mission. People question how academicians spend their time, and raise concerns about the availability of faculty to mentor and educate students. No longer is the institution revered as the place where minds are cultivated and developed for active participation in a democratic society. Parental and labor market conditions and pressures are the stimulants for focusing on employable skills at the completion of one's higher education (Patel, 1995). The intrinsic value of learning is not accentuated. Stakeholders are questioning what they are getting for their dollars.

For a state university, questions such as these are raised: Why is it essential or important to have a large number of out-of-state students? We are a state institution, and thus in-state students should occupy our classrooms. After all, whose parents work and live in the state and pay taxes? Why is the university research mission so time-absorbing and irrelevant to societal needs? Is such research conducted at the expense of educating undergraduate students? What contribution does research make to solving today's social ills?

These questions have refocused the public research university's attention on its mission and vision for the next century. Societal conditions such as escalating poverty, increasing family dysfunction, restructuring of the economy, the burgeoning underachievement rates among at-risk groups of youth, and the increasing inner-city decay have caused the public to question whether the current research agenda of the institution is balanced and, in some cases, appropriate. Perhaps universities have not done a good job of communicating the impact of the research function on quality-of-life issues and social conditions.

Public research institutions are also faced with fewer resources—which can be largely attributed to revenue constraints at the state level and a more competitive environment for securing grants and contracts from federal agencies. At the University of Michigan, we have tried to address this state of affairs by the notions of innovation by substitution (Whitaker, 1990) and responsibility center management (RCM). For the first concept, rather than seeking to achieve the growth by incremental resources for new programs and initiatives, one would eliminate or reduce current programs to redistribute resources for new efforts. The assumption of incremental budget increases at the rate of inflation is considered passé. More recently, the University of Michigan central administration adopted the second notion, RCM, as its new budgeting and management approach. Responsibility center management, like Michigan's VCM (Value Center Management), is a budget procedure for giving academic units (responsibility centers) more autonomy in the management of both revenues and expenditures. The University of Illinois, Urbana-Champaign, is also considering adopting this approach in this era of resource constraint. It would appear that within the next decade, public research institutions will manage their financial affairs in a manner more like that of private institutions.

Conclusion

Serving as dean at a large public research university requires one to function sandwiched between faculty and central administration and between internal and external affairs. One must also be responsible for fundraising and vision setting and be held accountable to a variety of constituencies. Few deans are trained to be managers. Organizational complexities and changes in public research universities add to the enormous challenge of leading, setting standards of excellence, and securing a position for schools of social work.

Throughout different stages of my academic and professional career, I have had the good fortune of having extremely competent mentors of both genders. However, more recently, my mentors have been male. When I arrived at the University of Michigan, I felt the need to expand my circle of mentors and thus asked for advice and guidance from a variety of people—all of whom were male. One has had a distinguished career as a fundraiser, raising literally millions of dollars, and is extremely knowledgeable about the management of resources and budgets. Another is keenly aware of the university's culture and its history and values and provides useful advice on our ideas and plans for the future. Another, outside the University of Michigan, knows nothing about the daily operations of the institution, but is a brilliant and competent leader, with a breadth of administrative experiences. Drawing upon each of these mentors' unique competence and understanding has been invaluable. Participation in all-women deans' groups has also been invaluable. Periodically, women deans have held summer retreats or special sessions in conjunction with annual meetings to discuss the role of dean and to mentor those who are new to the role. These sessions have been extremely helpful because participants share their most interesting challenges and feelings, and how they responded.

In conclusion, the personal experiences and observations contained in this chapter will hopefully invite reflections and comments from deans or those with aspirations to become a dean. Truly, the advancement of the social work profession will require thoughtful and courageous leadership. Deans are in a strategic position to develop that leadership.

References

Edward, R., and Baskin, F. "Providing leadership." In F. Raymond (ed.), *The Administration of Social Work Education Programs: The Roles of Deans and Directors*. National Association of Deans and Directors, 1995.

Patel, C. (ed.). *Reinventing the Research University*. Proceedings of a symposium held June 22–23, 1994. Los Angeles: University of California Office of the Vice Chancellor for Research, 1995.

Raymond, F. (ed.). *The Administration of Social Work Education Programs: The Roles of Deans and Directors*. National Association of Deans and Directors, 1995.

Videka-Sherman, L., Allen-Meares, P., and Yegidis, B. "Social Work Deans in the 1990s: Survey Findings." In F. Raymond (ed.), *The Administration of Social Work Education Programs: The Roles of Deans and Directors*. National Association of Deans and Directors, 1995.

Whitaker, G. *Enhancing Quality in an Era of Resource Constraints. Report of the Task Force on Costs in Higher Education*. Ann Arbor: University of Michigan, 1990.

PAULA ALLEN-MEARES is dean and professor in the School of Social Work at the University of Michigan, Ann Arbor.

*If you have been there and done it all, then you have a unique perch
on which to observe the ups and downs of deaning.*

Looking Back: Perspectives of a
Former Dean, Provost, and President

Thomas Ehrlich

As a dean at Stanford, and in subsequent administrative roles as provost at the
University of Pennsylvania and president of Indiana University, I found that
the success or failure of one's tenure turns on choosing the correct two or three
key goals, then sticking with them until they are accomplished. A few examples will illustrate the point.

The most important of a dean's goals will usually be academic—strengthening teaching, research, or both, in some particular way. At Stanford Law
School in 1971, when I became dean, I had just led a major revision of the
curriculum, and the academic enterprise was in strong shape. At that time,
the school had a first-rate faculty and student body, but they were housed in
a second-rate building. It had been a splendid structure when built in the
1890s, but it had not been renovated since. Therefore, raising funds for new
facilities, with additional funding for faculty endowment and scholarships, was
the obvious key priority. I led an aggressive and successful fundraising campaign
for three years and oversaw construction of new buildings in the next two. As a
result, I was able to achieve other objectives—particularly attracting and retain-
ing the key faculty—far more easily than otherwise might have been the case.

After taking a leave of absence from academe to serve as president of the
federal government's Legal Services Corporation, I returned to higher education at the University of Pennsylvania, where I served as provost for six years.
I worked closely with the deans of Penn's twelve schools, and was directly
involved in selecting a number of deans.

The provost or academic vice president is responsible for a university's academic enterprise. The provost works with deans and others to set key academic

NEW DIRECTIONS FOR HIGHER EDUCATION, no. 98, Summer 1997 © Jossey-Bass Publishers

priorities for the university as a whole, then does everything possible to help the deans strengthen their schools in ways that are consistent with those priorities. Every provost naturally wants his or her university to be more than the sum of its schools. So a wise dean will do as much as he or she can to position his or her school to help the university achieve those priorities—in fact, to be vital to the university's success in doing so.

· The most useful step a dean can take in working with a provost is to identify how the mission of the school benefits the whole university. It is always helpful to a university, of course, for its school to improve academically. When a school's reputation is enhanced, the university's reputation is also enhanced. But every effort should be made to think in terms of the university as well as the school. There is a reason why schools are clustered in universities rather than existing as freestanding entities. Each school is strengthened by being part of a university. Yet often school deans seem to reflect a limited grasp of the university perspective on a variety of issues. Wittgenstein wrote that "the fly in the bottle doesn't know the shape of the bottle." Deans need to get outside of the university bottle to understand its shape.

I was struck, in reading the account of "A Day in the Life of a Dean" in Chapter One, by a seeming lack of effort to do just that. The author approached his appointment with the academic vice president "with dread." He noted that "the academic vice president (AVP) and I do not get along well . . . and I feel strongly that he cannot effectively represent the needs of the deans to the administration"—presumably this means the president. Although the brief meeting relates to requests for financial support, which the AVP denies, the description does not reflect much of an understanding of the problems faced by the university or the AVP or how the school might help in addressing those problems. It is not surprising that the AVP does not show much sympathy. Some deans, as a matter of personal temperament, view relations with the university administration as a form of combat, particularly when the issue involved is money, as it so often is. Other deans, on the other hand, recognize that the best way to gain support is to offer support. Unfortunately, I sense a lack of this perspective in Chapter One.

Schools of social work have a unique lens through which to see and work with the communities around them. That lens can be of enormous value to a university. The University of Pennsylvania took seriously its responsibilities as a citizen of west Philadelphia. When I came to Penn, however, it seemed to me that the Penn School of Social Work and its dean had little concern about how, or even whether, the university met those responsibilities. The school had strong ties to scores of social service agencies in Philadelphia, but the dean had made little effort to help make them ties to the university as well as to the school. Fortunately, the new dean, hired while I was provost, completely changed the scene on this as well as other fronts.

I stress that these insights are from the perspective of a provost. Reading this volume, I was surprised at how little attention was paid to the reality that schools of social work differ not only from each other—a point that is recognized—but also, and more sharply, from the other schools in a university.

In any university, the school (or schools) of arts and sciences is at the heart of the institution. Many universities continue quite well without schools of law or social work, but no great university exists without an arts and sciences core. A basic issue for the dean of social work or any other professional school is how that school can help strengthen arts and sciences (and how arts and sciences can strengthen the school). As one example, I am committed to promoting community-service learning opportunities—particularly among undergraduates—to link academic study and community service through structured reflection in class discussions, journals, and papers. Faculty in social work have long been involved with their students in community service that is closely tied to their classroom work. Those faculty members can help their arts and sciences colleagues in the realm of community-service learning.

Deans of social work can also assist their decanal colleagues in other professional schools. At Penn the social work dean developed a number of strong interschool ties in teaching, research, and service that helped his school, other schools, and the university. Lawyers, doctors, nurses, and business people, for example, regularly work with social workers, as well as with each other. The schools that train those other professionals should take far more advantage than most do of the learning that can come from social work. That only happens, however, if the dean of social work is in the lead.

At Penn, I began an academic planning process to establish university objectives in general terms, then school-based plans that furthered the university objectives while enhancing each school, and finally to strengthen Penn as a whole in light of those plans. The process took six years, by the end of which all schools and the university as a whole had developed a continuous planning capability that served it well. University objectives and school plans were reviewed by a planning and budget committee that included faculty members chosen by the elected faculty leaders and deans and faculty members whom I had appointed. Some deans responded with enthusiasm to the planning process and sought to make the Penn slogan, "One University," an academic reality. Other deans resisted. Naturally, I was far more supportive of those who were seeking to enhance the entire institution.

My perspective changed somewhat, of course, when I moved from Penn to Indiana University. One is a private institution, with a primary obligation to academic excellence. The other must balance excellence with access, and has a primary obligation to serve an entire state and its citizenry. Penn has about twenty-four thousand students on one campus. Indiana University has about one hundred thousand students on eight campuses. The jobs of president and provost at the universities are also different. But in my case the difference was blurred because the Indiana University trustees hired me with a mandate to focus on academic issues. In their view, the university generally, and the Bloomington campus particularly, had been drifting a bit in academic terms.

My charge from the trustees was to stop that drift. Naturally, I turned for help to the chancellor and deans on each campus.

Even before I arrived in Indiana, I was told that the president must prepare the annual State of the University address, and that it was generally delivered in August, although that was the month I arrived. I responded that I knew little about the state of the university, but I would prepare a paper on "The University in the State," a play on words because one of my aims was to enhance the role of Indiana University in promoting the state's economic growth. That paper discussed the tensions involved in providing access to higher education while ensuring areas of real excellence. I sent the first and many succeeding drafts initially to deans, then to wider and wider groups of faculty and other advisors, seeking their counsel on the issues involved and attempting to garner their support. I even included the governor and other political leaders.

I recall clearly that some deans gave me detailed comments about the ways in which their schools were contributing—and might contribute more in the future—to the goals I had suggested. Several of those deans sharply criticized some points, but in the context of the university as a whole. Other deans, however, seemed defensive. Their responses were couched in terms of worries about how their schools might be overlooked or left behind. From that early interaction, I saw that some deans were simply unable to "get outside the bottle." I fear that their schools suffered as a result.

The paper, "Our University in the State," in its final form, was the initial step in an academic planning process that I began with a small group of deans and faculty leaders soon after I arrived at Indiana University. Naturally, the deans who had been most helpful at the outset were in that group. Ultimately, more than four hundred faculty members from all campuses, working in task forces, were involved in a yearlong collaboration. We wanted a comprehensive academic agenda for the entire university on all eight campuses, including more than eight hundred degree programs and the academic work of more than four thousand faculty members. We needed to be general in order to be comprehensive. At the same time, we wanted to avoid producing still another vague document full of puffed-up aspirations that could readily be ignored.

Our approach was to spell out specific initiatives, fifty-three in all, in three broad areas: undergraduate education, graduate education and research, and economic growth for the state of Indiana. For those initiatives, progress was mostly measurable quantitatively. The results were published as an ambitious agenda for strengthening the university in every academic aspect. We also published periodic progress reports on how well each campus and school was doing to achieve the goals of each initiative. Competition naturally arose among the campuses and schools. If one stalled on an initiative, the others' progress often acted as a spur. More important, each campus and school learned from the others.

I borrowed the Penn slogan and revised it for Indiana as "One University with Eight Front Doors." Some deans reacted with enthusiasm and sought to counteract the natural centrifugal pressures, both academic and political, within any academic institution of higher education, particularly when multiple campuses are involved. Others seemed more interested in shoring up the barriers that separated their schools from the rest of the university. Again, it should be no surprise that I tried to help the former group with a good deal more vigor than the latter.

One of the clearest differences among deans, at Indiana and at Penn, was that some could lead a planning process around key school priorities, whereas others seemed unable to even think about how to set those priorities. To the latter group, everything was important, and as a result all too often little happened to enhance the school. That group also was much more prone to be caught up in diversionary problems. Planning helps a dean focus on central goals and avoid spending time and energy on side issues.

Conclusion

I think it is important to have a formal review process for all academic administrators, including deans, presidents, and provosts. It makes sense, every five years or so, to ask a group of faculty, students, staff, and alumni to identify the administrator's strengths and areas for improvement. Done properly, the results can be helpful, though the process may include some tension.

Second, it is important for a dean to have an explicit agreement with the provost or president about returning to a full-time position. At Stanford, for example, the provost arranged with me and other deans that we would be paid an amount equal to the highest salary of a regular member of our school's faculty. We were also each promised a sabbatical year if we survived at least five years as dean. Apart from a real need for retooling, a former dean does a great favor to a successor to be away for at least a year.

Third, in my initial months as provost, I spent a day with each of several provosts at other institutions. I admired them and their work, and sought a short tutorial from each. They were flattered to comply, and in the process I learned a great deal. In retrospect, I should have done the same thing when I first became a dean. Each school and university is different, of course, and no lesson from one can be applied exactly to another. But there are important insights to be gained.

And finally, it was helpful to read the reports and other writings of my predecessors, and I gained a tremendous perspective on the jobs of Stanford dean, then Penn provost, and then Indiana University president in the process. My favorite Indiana predecessor, in fact, was David Star Jordan, who had left in the 1890s to become the first president of Stanford. My most vivid memory, however, is of reading the records of the first Stanford law dean at a time when I was feeling particularly oppressed by my position. He used to go around the law building each night removing light bulbs, lest they be stolen. Not everything was easier in the good old days.

THOMAS EHRLICH, former dean of the Stanford University Law School, is former provost of the University of Pennsylvania and former president of Indiana University. He is currently Distinguished University Scholar at California State University.

Where can one find a description of the joys of deaning? Look no further.

The Leadership Role of a Dean

Claire M. Fagin

Is a deanship, a deanship, a deanship? Reflecting on my fifteen years as dean of the University of Pennsylvania School of Nursing, and the experiences of three deans of Penn's school of social work, I would answer: Yes and no. In many ways the position of dean, no matter the school, has characteristics in common. In other ways, the size of the school and what its discipline is make for huge differences. The mix of disciplines and their varying degrees of prestige make a deanship different in many ways for the incumbent. The extent to which the discipline is understood by the university administration makes it easier—or harder—to fulfill the role successfully. The extent to which the public values the discipline is directly related to the ease of fundraising.

In all of these ways deans of schools of social work and nursing share problems and concerns. Certainly, in a university with a prestigious medical school, business school, and a large, multidepartment school of arts and sciences, all other schools must "measure up" for the deans to be considered equal players. That this can occur is a tribute to the dean, the faculty, and the administration.

However, differences aside, the similarities among deans' roles and stresses bring rare levels of camaraderie to the group of deans working together across discipline boundaries, as long as an atmosphere of competition for resources has not become the prevailing mood at the university.

The term *middleness* can be used to describe the role of deans. It is used in this volume as well. I was in the dean's role for some time before I saw myself as a person and position in the middle.

How I saw my role after I had just accepted the position of dean of Penn's School of Nursing late in 1976 became apparent when my husband and I were invited to a reception for Penn trustees and I met a very prominent

New Directions for Higher Education, no. 98, Summer 1997 © Jossey-Bass Publishers

trustee who was himself a noted academic. When we were introduced he said, "Oh, you're the woman who is going to take on the nursing faculty." I retorted, in not even half a second, "No, I think you've gotten that wrong. I'm going to take on the university on behalf of the nursing faculty." I was stunned by my response to this important person, but I knew then that I was right and the nursing faculty needed just that kind of attitude. Although the strength of the faculty increased phenomenally over subsequent years, I never veered from that view.

I have come to believe that the dean's role is hard to understand even for people close to the position. I left the deanship in 1992, after fifteen years of considerable success. Even at the very end I had experiences that made apparent the difficulty of valuing the multiple agendas the dean must achieve. For example, the faculty most frequently measures your achievement by what you accomplish first, for them, and second, for the school inside and outside. Only a few faculty members are aware of your own scholarly work; most don't know what you've published. This becomes more apparent when they come to feel that your recognition is no longer important for their recognition. So, in my early years, when my professional fame and fortune helped make the school and my colleagues more visible, they were more aware of what I was doing professionally than in later years. Unless an article appeared in the journals of their preference they would be unfamiliar with it or the fact that I was publishing regularly, somewhere. Many would be surprised by the progression of my CV.

The provost (I reported to six during my fifteen-year deanship) would be aware of my university roles of managing the school and its budget. But, depending on the provost, would be more or less aware of any other aspect of the deans' roles. Of course, the role in development became more important over the years, so both the later provost and the president were clear about the success of their deans in this important realm. The provosts who had been deans themselves were closer to the reality of the total role than others but still, because of their current position, tended to value what mattered to them most in making the university work. Further, the less they knew about your discipline the less they valued any discipline-related activities. For those of us in professional disciplines such as nursing and social work, these activities loom large and play an important role in our own lives, the development of our disciplines, and the prestige of our schools. Yet they play almost no part in our appraisals by university administrators.

Early in my deanship the school's administrative staff was most informed about the dean's schedule. But, as the school became larger and more complex, and all of us became very adept with computers and electronic mail, I found the staff more or less in the same position as others; that is, more aware of the dean's role as it related to theirs and less aware of other aspects. Preparation for speeches, the toll of travel, even things like the time changes of travel seemed to escape notice. A type of superwoman fantasy develops (I guess if you're lucky) where each person sees the dean's role from the standpoint of what each one wants of it, and evaluates it in terms of how well the dean does at their particular piece.

During my deanship and later as interim president of Penn, I found the development officers and my own administrative staff had the best idea of what the administrator does. In both instances the staff members were fully aware of the entire calendar and the compromises and stresses that went into making the schedules work. I have found that my administrative assistants over the years varied between people who were extremely protective because they were aware of my tendencies to accept too many commitments and to maintain an open-door policy almost to a fault, and those who believed I could and should do it all. Both were right.

In an institution such as Penn, development officers are crucial to the work of the dean. Development officers have been among my most relied-on colleagues. They are directly involved with scheduling time for themselves, so are very aware of the dean's full and complex role. I have been blessed with development officers who have successfully interpreted the goals and activities of development to other staff and faculty so that time for this is recognized by all as a major priority. Yet delegation of responsibilities to others was a problem. To delegate tasks to academic administrators, such as associate deans for academic programs, was rarely possible in the School of Nursing, because each had her own imperatives. And delegating to administrative support staff was often resented by faculty members who felt that the administrative staff was growing too powerful.

What does all this mean? It suggests that the dean's role is somewhat anomalous. For success in the school, it must go up, down, across, and out, and each part of the school and university must feel that it is getting full value from the dean. I have found that deans of professional schools have a harder time with these expectations, because our involvement in our professions is crucial to our reputations, the reputations of our schools, and the development of our fields. But the fact is, neither faculty nor administration likes an outside dean, yet for fundraising and leadership the dean must play a major outside role. How the dean reconciles these somewhat disparate demands seems to me to relate to the individual's clarity on what others see and value, recognition of the vital aspects of the role and responsibilities of dean in a particular university, and a honed balancing act.

From the standpoint of the inside role, every dean must start with the university statement of mission, and the degree to which the school has planned its own mission in concert with the university's overall mission. Most mission statements I read at Penn dealt with similar issues at different stages of development: research; undergraduate education; student financial aid for diversity and strength of the student body; cooperative ventures between departments and disciplines; strengthening of the school of arts and sciences as the center of scholarship for all schools; building the attributes of Penn's urban character; outreach to the Commonwealth of Pennsylvania, the nation, and the global environment. And to accomplish all these ends, reallocation of resources (and in our current world of downsizing) was essential.

To implement the mission, all departments in the university must develop strategies for themselves or to facilitate others' implementation. The successful leader undoubtedly has taken part in developing the university mission and has already drawn attention and comments about it from faculty. The mission and goals are integrating principles around which school and department groups must frame their own statements of mission and goals and strategies for accomplishing them. Naturally, these statements must be consonant with the overall university mission.

In developing the dean's outside roles, building a network of support is crucial. Although the network is important internally as well, building an influential acquaintanceship in the broad community is crucial for deans of schools such as nursing and social work. Not only must this network think well of the dean—a minor goal that some individuals find sufficient—this network must understand the discipline, recognize its importance, and be willing to speak for it in the community and in the university. Some of the individuals involved in this network must be part of the group viewed as powerful by the university administration and be part of the wide university "family."

In agreement with several writers herein I believe the dean exercises great influence in the school. But I see the dean's influence as threefold: areas where the dean influences, areas where the dean is directly involved, and areas where the dean is indirectly involved. The dean can influence others rather than act directly in many faculty and students matters: research and dissemination; appointments, promotion, tenure decisions; curriculum and student relations. Though there are individual and committee decisions in these areas, the dean's approval, support and—in the case of a very respected dean—opinions will make a difference.

The dean must be directly involved with others in strategic planning, development, budget planning and implementation, (in the case of nursing) salary decisions, leadership development, outreach, and public relations for the school and the profession. The dean is indirectly involved with other administrators who handle personnel management, including affirmative action, training of faculty and staff, physical plant maintenance, and other responsibilities. Although ultimately responsible for performance standards, I have always encouraged participation and decision making at each individual's highest possible level. I am known as somewhat ambiguous by some and for giving a long rope by others. I do get into the act for communication, conflict resolution, and supervision when needed.

I have often been asked: Why be a dean? Why remain a dean? Let me conclude by saying that the role of dean can be the most satisfying of all administrative roles in universities. Being the person in the middle is at once a stimulating challenge that, when accomplished, brings not only satisfaction but considerable power. The key is meeting the expectations and beyond of the various audiences who appoint and reappoint you and your ability to achieve balance among the constituents.

I have defined my role as providing leadership to the members of the school so that the mission of the school can be accomplished. I see my major function as developing leadership in others. That is the way I have assessed myself, in part because of the needs of the field. This function can only be done when leadership is democratic rather than autocratic and where those involved in carrying out the decisions are part of the decision-making process.

CLAIRE M. FAGIN, PH.D., R.N., is professor and former dean of the University of Pennsylvania School of Nursing and also former interim president of the University of Pennsylvania.

When it comes to academic leadership, what does it mean to be at the center or at the heart of an organization?

What Does a Dean Do?

Clarence G. Newsome

My youngest daughter asked me several years ago, "What exactly do you do, Daddy?" She was about seven at the time. "Well, honey," I began lightheartedly, perhaps a bit facetiously. "Daddy picks up paper, moves furniture, licks stamps . . ." Almost as an afterthought I continued, "teaches, writes papers, raises money, provides leadership for people who want to . . ." She interrupted, "What does picking up paper and moving furniture have to do with anything?" Instantly, all lightheartedness gave way to sobered reflection. It made me think, What is the connection?

Two years before, this same precocious daughter had raised one of the most challenging theological questions I have ever had to entertain. (I clearly remember thinking that, as the dean of a theological school, I was fortunate that this question had been raised at home and not in public.) She had asked me, "If Jesus is God, then where is God when Jesus is talking to God?" With this question resurrecting in my mind, I began to reflect on her current query in terms of roles. Perhaps the connection was that as dean I necessarily had to fill many roles, from maintenance man to religious scholar. Whatever the connection, she had managed to put her inquiring finger on an intellectual nerve.

What does a dean do? I have thought about this question incessantly since my daughter posed it. I have thought about it in some rather unconventional ways, particularly in the context of my own experience at the only predominantly African American theological school in America integrally related to a comprehensive research university, a context with role implications that extend far beyond the school and the university. These implications have often compelled me to raise the question of what a dean does in relation to the conceptual issues of identity and location. Function is clearly in question whenever identity and location are at issue. It is in question in the general sense of responsibilities, duties, tasks, and activities; in a more profound sense, it is in question in terms of effectiveness. What does a dean do that is effective and efficacious in the life of a school, and that redounds to the benefit of the university and the community at large? In my case, what does a dean do that benefits the African American church and community nationwide?

A similar question guided a seminar on denominational leadership that I led three years ago. Meeting intermittently over two years in various parts of the country, a group of denominational executives and I, in search of the meaning of effective leadership, discussed a number of books. To our pleasant surprise, Max DePree's book, *Leadership Jazz,* spoke succinctly, even poetically, to us. More loosely penned than the other books we examined, DePree's impressed us with its major points: a leader can resolve issues of identity and location by differentiating between the center of an organization and its heart, effectiveness can be determined by the leader's ability to identify what is worth measuring, and it can be measured to the degree that an organization can connect the voice of a leader to his or her touch.

Interestingly, DePree cites deans as leaders only to illustrate the point that an organization's center is not synonymous with its heart. "CEOs and members of Congress, and deans, by the nature of the power that accumulates around them, are at the center. They can't avoid it," he writes. However, "being at the center, being in control, differs from being at the heart" (p. 35). This is a most helpful distinction, one that I have found rings true to my own decanal experience.

At the center the dean derives his or her identity from the authority vested in the office to which he or she is appointed; at the heart the dean derives identity from the power that is voluntarily and informally conferred by the community; at the center his or her identity is mostly perceived and manifested abstractly and impersonally; at the heart it is regarded in concrete and personal ways, meaning that at the heart the dean's identity assumes the qualities of personality, qualities that give rise to the power of persuasion and influence. At the heart the dean fills the most important role of all, the personification of the core values of the school. At the heart the dean can fill many of the roles that characterize the life of the school because there he or she is fundamentally connected to them all.

When I arrived at the university ten years ago, an associate said to me, "If you can succeed here you can succeed anywhere." As he intended, I received his cryptic remark as both a challenge and encouragement. When I deciphered it, I realized that he had most trenchantly put his finger on a peculiarity of our university, where an informal infrastructure dominates organizational life. In such an environment the roles people fill are critical, though no role is more important than that of friend. In such a work environment, you have to rely heavily on who you know and how well you are known and personally liked to get things done. Getting results unavoidably pivots on familiarity, especially with clerical workers and other support personnel. My colleague seems to have intimated that if I could master the art of familiarity, of working within a highly informal infrastructure, then I could succeed anywhere. Advantages include the many favors that people are likely to do as an exercise of personal power "just for you." Disadvantages include institutionalized moodiness, which breeds heightened unpredictability concerning administrative timing, rhythm, and cadence, acutely ambiguous administrative policies and practices, and substandard connections among units, such as divisions, schools, departments, and among individuals in relation to information flow. In the final analysis, disadvantages include excessive institutional frustration.

According to DePree, an organization is best when the leader occupies the center and the heart simultaneously (p. 35). This appears to be an apt prescription for any organization where informal and formal infrastructures are out of balance. I certainly have found it imperative to orchestrate balance by aligning the center with the heart as consistently as possible. The process has, indeed, been much like DePree's analogy between leadership and jazz band leaders. "Jazz band leaders," writes DePree, "must choose the music, find the right musicians, and perform—in public" (pp. 8–9). They must do so with the understanding that "the effect of the performance depends on so many things—environment, the volunteers playing in the band, the need for everybody to perform as individuals and as a group, the absolute dependence of the leader on the members of the band, the need of the leader for the followers to play well." They must do so with the keen understanding that "jazz . . . combines the unpredictability of the future with the gifts of individuals."

As dean, I have embraced the vital importance of consciously and intentionally fusing the abstract with the concrete dimensions of my job, of personalizing my title by trying to choose the right tones and words for the school to express and project its mission; to find the right faculty, students, and staff or, more important, the roles that each can play best as faculty, students, and staff; do these things and much more in full view of the public. I have endeavored to do so to the end that each person in the life of the school, alumni and friends included, is inspired and motivated to draw on his or her unique gifts to contribute fully and collegially.

At all levels of the process, I have attempted to move people toward the realization of a common future that no vision statement can capture in detail or absolutely ensure. The net effect has been that of constantly moving to position myself in the life of the school where my voice can connect with my touch.

According to DePree, the connection of voice and touch is essential for measuring effectiveness and, more significantly, identifying what to measure. The identification of what to measure weighs heavily and immediately on the health of the school. Without a clear delineation of what actually counts, efforts to achieve balance between informal and formal administrative operations are futile and draining of both human and material resources. This is the case whether balance issues and concerns are mostly internal to the school or external in terms of the interaction of the school with the university. The dean must be most vigilant in attending to a school's well-being. In this regard, serving as guardian of the school's welfare may be the most critical leadership role a dean must fill. He or she must always be in the vanguard in matters of institutional health. Nothing signals the guardian role more clearly than the school's ability to experience the dean's voice connecting with his or her touch.

Among the things that are of greatest value in the life of a school are the media through which a dean's voice connects authentically with his or her touch. Authenticity is an important modifier because it calls attention to the fact that the element of human worth is foundational. The dean's voice must authentically connect with his or her touch because the community needs to trust that its members are fundamentally affirmed as human beings, whether they are responsible for maintenance or must produce great works of research. No truth is more glaring in the life of a scholarly community than the truth of one's humanity. The pursuit of truth through the enterprise of scholarship is no more noble than when it rises and proceeds within a context of affirming the humanity of faculty, students, staff, alumni, and friends alike. A clear sign of authenticity on the dean's part is the articulation of power through the voice of the heart and the exercise of authority with a personal touch.

DePree makes an uncontestable point when he asserts that "leaders make public promises" (p. 19). Deans must and do make public promises all the time. Even their visions for their schools are a form of a promise that must be kept if the school is to connect voice with touch and declare it authentic. As promise maker, the dean unavoidably assumes the role of a leader's leader to the faculty, and an exemplary leader to students, staff, alumni, friends, and supporters. The distinction is that in the first instance the dean leads the way in establishing a track record of promises worth defending. As DePree puts it, "the best leaders promise only what's worth defending" (p. 21). The dean should aspire to be the best leader in the school. A solid track record in making promises that are worth defending helps to establish this reputation by garnering the respect and support, if not always the admiration, of peers, faculty colleagues whose leadership is absolutely essential to fulfilling the school's mandate. It demonstrates a level of judgment and wisdom that evokes allegiance and commitment to team work. In the second instance, the critical point is that the dean serves as a model for making promises that are most often kept. For in keeping promises the dean demonstrates integrity and engages in an act of joyful accountability, that is, a way of showing esteem for others that results in a pattern of mutual respect and emotional well-being.

For all that deans must do to safeguard, promote, and capitalize on the collective intellectual intelligence of their schools, they have even weightier responsibility to do likewise in the interest of their school's collective emotional intelligence. In my opinion, this is often overlooked when considering a dean's duties. One of the most helpful points that Daniel Goleman makes in his recent book, *Emotional Intelligence,* is that intellectual capacity is minimized to the degree that emotional capacity is retarded or absent, to the extent that the capacity for self-control, self-motivation, zeal, and persistence are limited (p. xii). Too often the collective intellectual intelligence of a school is asynchronous to its emotional intelligence. Almost invariably, noncreative tension and conflicts can be traced to a deficit in emotional intelligence. Whether it emanates from an influential member of the group or not, it can be traced to a lack of self-control, minimal self-motivation, overzealousness, or too little persistence. An enormous amount of time and energy can be expended on issues that arise more from the affective rather than the cognitive domain. From my vantage point, members of the community are not necessarily unaware of this reality; they are too intellectually bright to be otherwise. But, because of apparent emotional limitations, they tend to be too inclined and content to let the dean bear the burden of being the one who is most balanced intellectually and emotionally.

The school expects the dean, as leader, to fill the role of the most balanced person in the community, this is not an ill-founded or misguided hope. In its own way and on its own terms the community is deeply aware of the importance of having a balanced person in the leadership role. I long ago concluded that the community has a right to expect that the dean will be a bellwether for intellectual and emotional balance.

There is a soul to the life of a school that expresses itself in the form of community spirit. There is a fragility to the soul that must be well attended foremost by the dean if the spirit is to be upbeat, positive, vigorous, energetic, lively, buoyant, inviting, and appealing. The organic character of a school emanates from a life force that is greater than the sum of its membership. This intangible quality can easily atrophy if not nurtured through sacrificial, sometimes thankless, service on the part of the dean. In many respects it is through self-giving, the role of servant leadership as John Greenlief calls it in a book by that title, that the dean primarily feeds the collective mind of the school and thereby occupies not merely its center but its heart; it confirms that the connection between voice and touch is authentic. In a tangible way, confirmation of the dean on the part of the school opens the way for growth quantitatively and qualitatively, even when a school is faced with budget reductions and retrenchment.

During each of the first five years of my deanship, the university reduced the school's budget. In the fourth year, the school was compelled to lay off staff members as the university retrenched. The severance of employees was particularly painful for the school, painful to the core of its soul. Many people had developed intimate and caring relationships with some individuals whose positions were terminated. Yet, through the pain, a level of confirmation of leadership remained that enabled private funding to increase, enrollment to grow, and a greater sense of cooperation to develop. I should like to think that a willingness to give myself completely to the care of the school from the outset of my deanship, to the care of its soul at all times, and especially in the face of being second-guessed and questioned, even doubted, proved to be the essential difference. For when I called on others to do more to help address the crisis, people chose to work beyond differences of opinion to keep the school strong, to keep its spirit vigorous.

Of the innumerable challenges that a dean encounters, none is more strategic than leveraging the spirit of a school for growth. If there is any opportunity for a dean to reap what he or she sows, in the most positive sense of this expression, it is that of clearing the way for the spirit of the school to generate institutional momentum. Typical of this momentum is the kind of creative energy that fuels expansion numerically, and in ways that substantially add to the school's communal life. Energy, like life, draws energy to itself. An energetic faculty and student body will draw outstanding faculty and students. Outstanding faculty and students will draw substantial support from alumni and friends.

Expectations have long been high in African American churches and communities that the school over which I preside will produce religious leaders of the highest quality. This cannot be achieved without substantial support and resources. For this reason, the connection between the dean's activity in clearing the way for the spirit of a school and its energy level cannot be minimized.

Clearing the way, however, is not easy. In fact, a dean can incur much pain trying to do so. Sometimes it cannot be accomplished without heroic forbearance and internal fortitude. In this connection, DePree's contention that "a leader needs to have a high threshold of pain and low tolerance for" utter foolishness, is quite germane (p. 200). There are times when deans must act as institutional police, protecting the life of the school from those "crimes of the spirit—cynicism, destructive criticism, unnecessary conflict, personal animosity, gossip"—that pollute the atmosphere and lead to a kind of spiritual asphyxiation (p. 203).

Clearing the way is itself a gift a dean can make to the spirit of a school. But is only one among many that the dean can present as the chief gift bearer. Others include a willingness to honor the school's heart with a commitment to intimacy (even when an institution is already bent toward familiarity), a commitment to lead from the center and heart with dignity and civility, a commitment to embrace the perspectives of others, and above all to encourage freedom of speech and critical inquiry.

In the final analysis, the dean fulfills the roles best by realizing that neither the center nor the heart of a school are meant to be places of confinement; and that it is not the dean's role to either dominate the dialogue of the school or to lead with an autocratic hand. For me, the dean is at his or her best when extending upward and outward beyond the center and the heart, to speak and to be spoken to, to touch and to be touched in the interest of bonding with those he or she is appointed to serve. By means of bonding, the reality of the school is transformed by the truth it pursues as a scholarly community. It is transformed into a haven for healing, "a place where work becomes redemptive, where every person is included," a place where every person can move in the direction of wholeness and the fullness of his or her humanity (p. 63ff).

What does a dean do? A dean endeavors to move the center of a school to its heart, a position where the dean's voice can best connect with his or her touch. From the vantage point of the heart, the dean attempts to assume myriad roles in an authentic way, among them: guardian of the school's welfare; maker of public promises; promoter of emotional intelligence; exemplar of intellectual and emotional balance; servant leader; protector and leverager of the school's spirit. Ultimately, the dean fills the role of chief emotional intelligence gift bearer, the one who presents uncommon commitment to such values as intimacy, dignity, civility, shared perspectives, and freedom of speech and inquiry, values that signal a visible, vibrant, pulsating, and palpable community of learning and scholarship.

References

DePree, M. *Leadership Jazz*. New York: Bantam Doubleday, 1993.
Goleman, D. *Emotional Intelligence*. New York: Bantam Doubleday, 1995.

CLARENCE G. NEWSOME is dean of the Howard University School of Divinity.

Understanding the phenomenal pace and direction of change in our society is essential for deans devoted to advocating for change inside academe.

The Dean as Advocate for Change

John J. McCoy

Forces for change in engineering education can be traced to sources external to the campus. These forces are placing new demands on the role of deans of engineering, especially the need to assist faculty with responses to changes from beyond the campus. The task is relatively easy and pleasant during times of expansion and growth; however, it becomes a major challenge when resources are stagnant and decreasing.

Four major changes in the larger society are affecting engineering education. These are (1) the change in American corporate culture in response to fears about global competition; (2) the dramatic drop in the number of American students aspiring to careers in engineering and science; (3) the change in funding of academic engineering research; and (4) the globalization of engineering research and design. As an educator and engineer, not an expert on the forces shaping society, I make no claim as to the comprehensiveness of this list of changes. The significance of their impact, however, becomes self-evident when an engineering school dean advocates for responses to these major changes.

Change in American Corporate Culture

Over the last several decades, corporate America has experienced fundamental changes in meeting the challenge of competing in a global economy. Corporate downsizing and structural changes in administration are to be seen not as isolated events, but as manifestations of changes affecting every aspect of corporate operations. The very culture of corporate America has undergone change, and this change is influencing the characteristics deemed most desirable when hiring engineering graduates. The work ethic and sequential reasoning skills, hallmarks of engineering education, remain much appreciated skills. However, in a buyer's market, industry is demanding more and is seeking to bring this message to engineering educators, often through the persons of the deans. It has been a remarkably consistent message throughout my eight-year tenure as dean.

There has always existed a tension between industry's desire for technical skills training and the engineering school's commitment to educating a well-rounded engineer. In an earlier time the tension was often seen in terms of a more scientifically literate faculty in conflict with an industry's need for designers to accomplish specific tasks. This earlier tension, however, largely vanished as the half-life of any particular technology became short when compared to the career-life of the design engineer. The necessity of a strong foundation in mathematics and science in the presence of rapidly changing technology has been accepted, for some time, by the forward-looking high-tech industries that rely on engineering graduates.

A more recent tension can be seen in the efforts of industry to promote horizontal integration and the traditional vertical structure of engineering curricula. Horizontal integration takes place when design is linked to engineering and scientific research, and in the processes by which design becomes a product and the product becomes a profit. Typical engineering curricula reflect a vertical structure that isolates both the individual student and the subject matter in sequential knowledge acquisition. The tension between the vertical structure of engineering education and the horizontal structure of an integrated corporate culture calls for a broader definition of engineering than simply incorporating the advances of science into improved product designs. Addressing this tension can lead to the development of a more broadly educated graduate with a greater appreciation for lifelong learning. The success of an engineering school will depend, in part, on how well the dean can interpret for the faculty the relationship between changing corporate cultures and the need for innovative approaches to engineering education.

Changing Aspirations of American Students

After a significant increase in the number of undergraduates studying engineering in the early 1980s, total enrollment has declined for a decade. One result has been increased competition among schools of engineering to attract students from a decreasing applicant pool. It is clear that, to reverse this downward trend, engineering schools must place greater emphasis on attracting a diverse student population. The traditional pool of white males with an aptitude for mathematics and science, looking to be the first or second generation in their family to attend college in the search for a good job, is simply too small.

It is unfortunate that the image that most high school students have acquired is one in which engineering is viewed as narrow and unsatisfying, which is not the experience of most professional engineers. This image has been fostered by rigid engineering curricula standards, which allowed little flexibility for individual institutions to reflect their own educational philosophy, or individual students to express their own career objectives. The decreasing applicant pool is exerting strong pressure to change the engineering curricula and the mode of instruction. A heterogeneity across engineering schools, barely evident less than a decade ago, is now being celebrated as a strength of the American educational system.

In establishing criteria for accrediting programs of engineering, the Engineering Accreditation Council has accepted a comprehensive definition of engineering that reflects the totality of engineering practice. The new criteria are much more open. They challenge the faculty of each school to formulate a coherent undergraduate experience that is consistent with the school's educational philosophy and mission. Schools of engineering are now able to broaden their appeal in their efforts to attract a diverse student body.

The challenge facing schools of engineering is to seize the opportunities created by a vastly broader vision of engineering education. In small schools committed to undergraduate and graduate education, the task of guiding the change process will fall, by default, to the dean. In large schools exclusively focused on undergraduate education or schools with large faculties, the dean has the luxury of delegating to others the responsibility for keeping abreast of the forces of change.

Change in the Funding of Academic Engineering Research

Approximately one-fifth to one-third of schools of engineering have a commitment to academic research and graduate study. For the remainder, academic research is secondary to the main task of undergraduate teaching, albeit still valued for keeping the faculty current. With a number of notable exceptions, those schools of engineering committed to academic research are part of larger universities offering academic programs on all degree levels and in a broad range of disciplines.

Throughout the cold war, academic engineering research shared with mathematics and the physical sciences the federal government's generous support. Justified by its contribution to national security, the research on university campuses was left largely to the faculties of engineering and science. Peer review was practiced and critical evaluation using a criterion of "good science" was encouraged. The task of transferring the knowledge base achieved by academic research, especially to military application, was left to others.

The system worked remarkably well, as measured by the outcome of the cold war and the tremendous advances in critical technologies. Moreover, it has been a boon to several generations of academics able to take part in the research. The universities have benefitted significantly from the financial resources allowed for administering and housing the research. Two potential downsides of the support have been an unsustainable growth in the number of academics involved in the research, and a substantial reordering of university priorities as reflected in the reward system for these academics. Greatly reduced teaching loads for faculty charging large portions of their salaries to external sponsorship have become the mark of successful academic careers.

Fundamental change in the support of academic research in engineering and science began before the collapse of the Soviet Union. The same fear of global competition facing American business that prompted change in the corporate culture also led to changes in the relationship between government and universities, changes intended to maintain the nation's technological edge. Funding agencies, such as the National Science Foundation, began to shift dollars previously allocated for basic research to a more directed research. Moreover, because directed research has an identifiable payoff, it made sense to leverage the dollars allocated by the funding agency by requiring matching funds. The match would be provided by industry, by state legislatures in the case of public universities, and by whatever resources were available to private universities. One result is that private sector universities are generally participating less in academic engineering research than public sector universities. A second result is the rising importance of shorter timeframes for conducting research, as a criterion for evaluating proposed research. "Good science" is no longer the overriding criterion for evaluating academic research.

The end of the cold war has led to reduced public support for military-oriented research. With reduced dollars to support research, the funding agencies of the Department of Defense can be expected to target, even more carefully, the allocation of scarce resources. It is clear that university-based research in engineering and science must reflect more applied objectives in contrast to the tradition of basic research. As a result, the university is faced with a difficult choice: focus on "good science," even if this requires a retrenchment in the size of the activity, or accept a definition of academic research that can accommodate the shorter time horizon required when determining its potential for fostering an identifiable technology. Although changes in the funding of academic engineering research may not directly relate to curricula or modes of instruction, they do affect the hiring of faculty, faculty job descriptions, and faculty reward systems. Indirectly, then, the impact on every activity of the school will be profound. The need is to achieve a consensus not only in the faculty of engineering but also in the larger university.

Globalization of Engineering Design

The global transfer of jobs from a high-salaried work force to one that is less costly need not be restricted to manufacturing. In the past, product design and development have been accomplished exclusively in high-tech societies, only because the technological knowledge underlying these activities was located in these societies. The capability of instantaneously communicating this knowledge worldwide will allow corporations to export many of the design and development tasks to a less costly engineering work force. Even if the transfer is to a somewhat less efficient work force, the reduced cost of labor frequently dictates the decision.

Of course, the explosive growth of the communications and information industry is resulting in demands for a range of new technologies that can only increase the career possibilities for engineers. The outlook for graduates of schools of engineering should be very bright. However, the brightest career opportunities for the next generation of engineers will be available only to those able to accept a broad definition of the profession and lifelong learning. The pressures on schools of engineering to modify their curricula to meet these new demands of the marketplace will continue.

Conclusion

In the presence of societal pressures for change in the curricula content and the operations of a professional school, the dean must serve as the interpreter of those pressures and as an advocate for change. It is clear that changes related to American corporate culture, the career aspirations of entering college students, research funding sources, and the globalization of engineering design will profoundly affect the nature of engineering education.

JOHN J. MCCOY is professor and former dean in the School of Engineering at the Catholic University of America.

CONCLUSION

This volume addresses some of the issues and experiences of professional school deans. In some ways, it raises more questions than it answers. For example, it is not clear how the experiences of professional school deans differ from those of the deans of arts and sciences schools. It is clear that arts and humanities departments have different needs and interests from science departments with their large investments in research laboratories. Similarly, the title of dean is also used to designate administrative roles such as the deans of admissions, deans of students, and deans of continuing education. These administrative deans probably have more in common with other university administrators than they do with deans of professional and arts and sciences schools.

Each of the chapters in this volume identifies a different aspect of the dean's leadership role. However, they reflect more commonality than difference. Does the role of an engineering school dean differ substantially from that of a nursing school dean? Does the professional school deanship in a private university differ substantially from the same role in a public university? These questions call for further exploration. In this volume, however, it is clear that the deanship role includes such recurring themes as managing time, communicating with different cultures, guiding organizational change, raising money, promoting scholarship, engaging in self-reflective practice, keeping a perspective on your role and influence, navigating complex systems, effectively managing-up, pausing to reflect on the joys of the position, and advocating for change.

There are other issues facing deans of professional schools. There are two that relate to the career of a dean; namely, how deans are selected, and how they are educated to assume and successfully sustain the responsibilities of a deanship. For example, some business schools have searched outside the traditional academic marketplace to locate potential candidates for their deanships. The rationale for such efforts is based on a desire to find a seasoned manager with fundraising interests and abilities. These interests and skills are not usually found in large supply in the ranks of traditional academics. However, the vast majority of professional school deans are expected to continue to come from the ranks of the faculties. The biggest dilemma for search committees is assessing the capacities of faculty, who have distinguished themselves on campus as independent teachers and researchers, to assume roles that require the ability to work together with others on and off the campus. Very few faculty who have distinguished themselves through solo practice have opportunities to acquire the competencies related to contributing through others. The most promising professional school deanship candidates usually can demonstrate an ability to articulate a comprehensive understanding of the academic and practice environments and how the pieces fit together, to shift from maximizing personal contributions to maximizing the work of others, to build networks with people outside their immediate responsibilities and use those networks to accomplish shared goals, to become involved in the development of other people and to promote teamwork, to remove barriers to group problem solving, and to understand human motivation through the use of well-developed interpersonal skills.

The process of locating deanship talent is also complicated by the lack of faculty experience and skill in conducting dean search processes. There is a growing interest in the idea of involving experienced executive search firms in the management of the deanship search. Some schools have had success in using such firms with the traditional faculty search committee serving in more of an advisory role until the top list of candidates is presented for review and prioritizing. A future area of inquiry would be to study those professional schools that used outside search firms and to compare those experiences with the traditional campus approaches.

With or without search firms, finding deanship candidates with the following competencies is not easy: an ability to exercise significant leadership over decisions that affect the school, to shift from what is best for a group to what is best for the whole school, to help shape the future directions to be taken by the school, to obtain resources and build alliances that help the school, and to help shape the larger environment in ways that help the school survive and thrive. Future research is needed to determine if these are the core abilities for all professional schools or just for some of them, for public versus private universities, and for laboratory-based professions (medicine and engineering) versus nonlaboratory professions. In essence, although the deanship is a leadership position, the unique culture and environment of each profession may help to define the unique administrative abilities needed for the role of dean.

And finally, the questions remain as to how best to orient and educate deans over time. Although there are various executive development programs around the country related to managing nonprofit organizations, more attention is needed in the area of career development experiences for deans. Each profession has one or more professional associations that could sponsor such executive development training activities. Deans in their first few years of deanship experience may need very different types of learning experiences than those who have been on the job for five to ten years. The peer support group described in this volume represents a nontraditional approach to fostering greater understanding of the roles, responsibilities, and opportunities of the deanship. Some institutions are offering deans opportunities to receive coaching from specialists related to presentation skills, fundraising solicitation, and organizational change. Other institutions have developed personnel policies that limit the term of a deanship; for example, a twelve-year maximum based on a seven-year term with performance review, and then a five-year term. Further exploration of career development and administrative tenure is needed in order to better understand the nature of the professional school deanship.

As noted in the Editors' Notes at the beginning of this volume, the goal of the editors was to provide "live reports from the front lines" of academic administration. It is the hope of all of the authors that the readers will find useful perspectives, techniques, or questions that might help them become more reflective practitioners as administrators in higher education.

Michael J. Austin
Frederick L. Ahearn
Richard A. English
Editors

MICHAEL J. AUSTIN is professor in the School of Social Welfare at the University of California, Berkeley and dean emeritus of the School of Social Work at the University of Pennsylvania.

FREDERICK L. AHEARN is professor and dean emeritus at the National School of Social Services, Catholic University of America, Washington, D.C.

RICHARD A. ENGLISH is dean of the School of Social Work at Howard University, Washington, D.C.

INDEX

ORDERING INFORMATION

NEW DIRECTIONS FOR HIGHER EDUCATION is a series of paperback books that provides timely information and authoritative advice about major issues and administrative problems confronting every institution. Books in the series are published quarterly in Spring, Summer, Fall, and Winter and are available for purchase by subscription and individually.

SUBSCRIPTIONS cost $54.00 for individuals (a savings of 35 percent over single-copy prices) and $90.00 for institutions, agencies, and libraries. Standing orders are accepted. New York residents, add local tax for subscriptions. (For subscriptions outside the United States, add $7.00 for shipping via surface mail or $25.00 for air mail. Orders *must be prepaid* in U.S. dollars by check drawn on a U.S. bank or charged to VISA, MasterCard, or American Express.)

SINGLE COPIES cost $22.00 plus shipping (see below) when payment accompanies order. California, New Jersey, New York, and Washington, D.C., residents, please include appropriate sales tax. Canadian residents, add GST and any local taxes. Billed orders will be charged shipping and handling. No billed shipments to post office boxes. (Orders from outside the United States *must be prepaid* in U.S. dollars by check drawn on a U.S. bank or charged to VISA, MasterCard, or American Express.)

SHIPPING (SINGLE COPIES ONLY): $20.00 and under, add $3.50; to $50.00, add $4.50; to $75.00, add $5.50; to $100.00, add $6.50; to $150.00, add $7.50; over $150.00, add $8.50.

ALL PRICES are subject to change.

DISCOUNTS FOR QUANTITY ORDERS are available. Please write to the address below for information.

ALL ORDERS must include either the name of an individual or an official purchase order number. Please submit your order as follows:
   Subscriptions: specify series and year subscription is to begin
   Single copies: include individual title code (such as HE82)

MAIL ALL ORDERS TO:
   Jossey-Bass Publishers
   350 Sansome Street
   San Francisco, California 94104-1342

FOR SUBSCRIPTION SALES OUTSIDE OF THE UNITED STATES, contact any international subscription agency or Jossey-Bass directly.